Maneuvering Through the Adventure of Life

By

Salvatore Ferraro

Copyright © 2012 Salvatore Ferraro
All rights reserved.
ISBN-13: 978-1475134391
ISBN-10: 1475134398

Dedication

I dedicate this book to Lori, Nick, and Lili.

Lori, my wife, has made this book possible; without her support and love, this adventure would not have been attainable.

To Nick and Lili, my children, my inspiration, you can achieve anything you want in life.

Cover Picture

Salvatore Ferraro took the cover picture on his trip to Whistler Mountain, Vancouver. He had just skied down through the trees. He took the picture going back up the mountain from the chair lift.

This image was also the inspiration for the title of the book.

Skiing through the trees, being forced to take a different path then intended, not knowing the direction you are headed. Then reaching an opening and looking back to realize what you just accomplished.

A lot like life.

Table of Contents

1) *What is Needed to Succeed 1*
2) *Dreams / Childhood 19*
3) *Faith / Attitude Adult.......................................39*
4) *Planning / Meeting Lori 57*
5) *Sacrifice / Moving 77*
6) *Alternative plan / Moving Back to NJ 99*
7) *Giving / Motorcycle / Kidney 127*
8) *Reward / Doctorate / Trip 159*
9) *Wrap-Up..185*

Foreword

What do you want to achieve in your life: money, fame, time, or power? The secret to success is simple. The question you need to answer; "What are you willing to give up to achieve success?" You cannot achieve success if you are not willing to give something up, such as time, sleep, money, sport activities, and so on. Everything comes at a cost. Once you have made that choice and commitment to your goals, you can start to work on reaching your goals. Set small achievable steps, as there will be obstacles along the way that you must overcome.

This book illustrates a path or idea that will allow you to work toward your goals. You do not have to be rich or come from a place of prominence to be successful; it just requires commitment and hard work. My hope is that understanding how I achieved my goals will help you achieve your goals.

I grew up in a middle-class family, where both my parents worked to make ends meet. We were neither rich nor poor. We took a vacation every year and never wanted for anything. My parents struggled to provide my siblings and me with a normal middle-class life. I was an average student, getting mostly C's in grammar school and high school, not caring much about schoolwork, nor putting much effort into it. I just wanted to get through school. I never excelled at anything, nor was horrible at anything.

I graduated high school, once again in the middle of the pack. The Monday after graduation, I started to work at a full-time job. I thought I knew better than all my friends that went to college. I was working full time making money while my friends were going to college. Then reality set in, I was to be married and needed to support my wife and future family. I started looking for ways to make more money and find a better job. Would you believe that you needed a college education to get a higher paying job? This was the beginning of a twenty-four-year adventure, learning many lessons along the way, and earning my doctorate degree.

Over the past twenty-four years, my wife and I had many great joys and challenges. The biggest joys are our two children. A few of the challenges we have overcome are unemployment, living in three different states, numerous surgeries, dealing with death, and bankruptcy. Together, my wife and I have overcome these challenges and have prospered. This book covers these challenges plus others that we have endured. This book is for the average person who does not know what they want or how to achieve it. Taking one day at a time, having a positive attitude toward life, and hard work will provide the groundwork for you to succeed.

Each chapter of this book has four sections. The first section of each chapter highlights an event I experienced with the choices that I made, followed by a second section (Lessons Learned) explaining how I applied lessons learned to help overcome obstacles. The third section contains motivation concepts (Exercises). The fourth section is an area to take notes (Notes).

Ask yourself, how old are you going to be in five years? You are going to be five years older whether you accomplish your goals or not. Why not start working on your goals now?

Chapter 1

What is Needed to Succeed

- *Where are you in Life?*
- *Where do you want to go?*

What does motivation mean to you? All people have their own ideas and feelings on what motivation is to them. Different things motivate different people, some want money, some want power, and others want more time. Because many people want different things, I do not believe there is one method of motivation for everyone. This book is not about how to make money or become famous, unless that is what you want. This book shows you how to achieve anything you want from life, whether it is fame, fortune, or more time to spend with your family. There are numerous books written on the subject. My suggestion is to read as many as possible to find the ones that will motivate you. (There is a list of books for suggested reading at the end of this book).

The secrets to achieving your goals or dreams are to understand that you must give something up to make your goals or dreams come true. If you wish for something to happen, it will not happen. Checking your mailbox every day for a new job, a raise, or for whatever you desire will only result in disappointment. You must decide how important your goals and dreams are and what you are willing to give up to achieve them. In some cases, the sacrifice is not worth the reward. You need to make a commitment to yourself that you will achieve your goals and dreams. Becoming successful is a life and mind change. Ask yourself, what I am willing to change in my life to get what I want.

The first question you need to ask yourself is what do I really want? This is not as easy as it sounds. What is going to drive you when things get tough? What do you want in life? I suggest you spend a lot of time thinking about this. Think about the results, once you have the item you want. How is this going to change your life? Can you see yourself with this item or doing the activity you want? If you want a new car go to a car dealer and test-drive a new car. If you want a bigger home, go to an open house of your dream home. Then decide how hard you are willing to fight for it.

You cannot talk about motivation without mentioning the work of Abraham Maslow. In 1943, he proposed the idea of a "Hierarchy of Needs." The theory states there are five levels of basic needs a person must achieve. The five levels are physiological, safety, social/love, self-esteem, and self-actualization. Maslow believed that a person must achieve each level before moving on to the next level.

The physiological needs consist of the most basic: warmth, shelter, and food. These are the basic functions of humankind—the need to eat and have shelter. These needs are one of the biggest reasons why people work: to buy food and have shelter. A person must have these needs met or even exceeded before moving on in life. If a person is living paycheck to paycheck, there is no extra money for other toys in life.

The next level in Maslow's hierarchy is safety. This level includes items such as employment and health. At this level, people are not worried about where the next paycheck is coming from. They are in a healthy state of mind and body.

The third level, social/love, deals with love and belonging. In this stage, the person has a need of belonging. Having a group of friends or being in a relationship accomplishes this. This level helps with support and encouragement.

Level four is the esteem level, the need to be accepted by others. Each person should have self-esteem and self-respect. Each person needs to have a sense of contribution. This level is important in order to succeed at the highest level of success.

The last level is self-actualization. At this level, people can ask what they want to be in life. Once all the other levels are achieved this frees people to concentrate on what they really want in life. They will be able to concentrate on making it happen.

Maslow's Hierarchy of Needs is important to understand, at least at a basic level. Some people may never achieve the highest level for many different reasons. But you should realize that no matter what level you achieve, it affects your attitude and affects what you are capable of dreaming. As I look back on my life, I can now see why I did what I did. Understanding where you are in life will help you to decide what you need.

Several methods, not just one method, will help you to succeed down the path you choose. This book will provide a summary of different methods that could help you to succeed, methods that have worked for others and me. This book reviews what I have done over my life and how I applied these methods to help achieve my goals and dreams.

When I was growing up, I did not know what I wanted to be or do. I let life decide my path of travel; it was not bad, but it was not good either. I had no plans, nor did I even know I needed plans; no one ever told me that I should make a plan and follow it. I grew up pretty much doing what I wanted, when I wanted, within my financial constraints. It was not until I got married that I thought there had to be a better way then living paycheck to paycheck. I started looking at "get rich" schemes and reading different books on the subject—they all wanted money before giving out the secrets of success. I finally found a system that I thought would work for me: the "Think and Grow Rich" system.

This system consisted of a book and a workbook. The idea was to read the book and complete the workbook with my ideas. I must admit that I did not want to do all the things in the book. I did not feel that I needed to do everything. I treated the concepts presented more like a buffet. I chose the concepts that I liked. The important thing to keep in mind is to choose enough of the concepts to succeed.

"The difference between a successful person and others is not lack of strength, not lack of knowledge, but rather in a lack of will."
Vince Lombardi

Embrace certain traits to become successful. Very few people know what it takes to be successful. We do not have to be born with what it takes to be successful; we can learn from others what it takes to be successful. This section covers some of the major traits that I believe a person needs to be successful. I have put these traits to use to achieve some of my goals.

Attitude

Attitude is one of the most important traits leading to success. The right attitude will help you succeed; the wrong attitude will create failure. If you have the right attitude, you can achieve anything you set your mind to. Attitude is how you observe and react to different situations you encounter. No matter what happens, you must try to find the "silver lining" in everything. Your attitude must come from within. You cannot rely on others to set your attitude or you will be at the mercy of others and will never have complete control of your goals. How you create your attitude is difficult, and it is something that you must learn to control and create. Work on creating a positive attitude every day, and change the way you think of everything.

A positive attitude comes from practice and hard work. This is the foundation for your success. In today's world, there is a lot of negative information on television. It will require thought and planning to have a positive attitude. It will require you to think about everything you know. You must learn to look and rethink everything and search out the positive.

Often you will not see the positive aspect of a situation, but if you look hard enough you will find it.

How do you view Monday? Most people look at it as the end of the weekend and the beginning of the workweek. It is a time for you to look at what you did not finish last week, what you will finish this week, and it is a chance to start over. New opportunities will become available. You need to see this every week. Monday's should not be a depressing day, but a day to look forward to—a day to learn and accept new opportunities.

Desire / Persistence

How bad do you want your goal? Desire is the amount of grief that you are willing to deal with to get to your goal. People will ridicule some of your ideas. Are you going to be able to stand up for what you believe? Are you going to stay up late, take vacation days from work and make this an important part in your life? Or are you going to let life get in the way of your dreams?

"Victory belongs to the most persevering."
Napoleon Bonaparte

Faith

Faith is a state of mind, but is something that you can control. To start, you must have faith in yourself. If you do not believe in yourself, then no one will believe in you. You must believe that you will finish what you started. Some days you will ask, why am I putting myself through this? I will never finish. You need to have the faith in yourself that you can complete the task. If you do not have the faith in yourself, then you need to believe in something, such as religion. This will get you through the hardest times during your journey.

Knowledge

You are going to need to know something about what your goal is. Do research on your goal; discover what it will take to achieve what you want. Does your goal require special training? If you do not have the knowledge required, get it. Read or go to seminars. Knowledge will set you apart from others. Become an expert in the field that you are interested in.

Planning

Planning provides the means by which you will accomplish your goals. Having a plan helps in different ways. Firstly, it keeps you on track. Secondly, you know how far you need to go. Thirdly, it tells you how much of your goal is left. A plan will help you accomplish your goals. You need a basic plan in order to start to achieve your goals. Do you need to take a class, learn a trade, or obtain additional schooling? I am not talking about planning your whole life, but making small plans to start. Never compromise the goal; however, the plan can change in order to meet your needs.

Reward system

A reward system or incentive system keeps you motivated. Giving yourself a small reward will make the journey a little better. Once you reach milestones or interim goals, go out and celebrate. If you achieve a small goal, go out to dinner or buy something small. When you reach your major goal, make a bigger reward. Take a trip or buy something big. Relate the reward and accomplishment to each other.

If you have spare time, look at million dollar homes, or $200,000 cars. Experience what you want. This will provide two things: a needed break and a desire to continue.

Success through failure

During your lifetime, some issues will cause you to fail. Many times, they will be out of your control. Every person deals with these in different ways, but how you react to failure will determine your success. Two famous people that have failed during their lifetime were, Thomas Edison and Babe Ruth. Thomas Edison's most well-known invention was the light bulb, which provides light throughout the world. However, the development of this invention came with many failed attempts. I do not know the exact number of failures, but it ranged from 3,000 to 9,000 failures. His response to those failures was that they were not failures but ways not to make a light bulb. His attitude is what kept him going. Babe Ruth was known as the home-run king. He hit

714 home runs in his career. He also had the most strikeouts—over 1,300. This means he struck out twice as many times as he hit home runs. Many said he was the only person playing the game that swung for a home run every time he was at bat. His attitude was all or nothing.

Time management

Utilizing your time wisely is important for you to achieve your goals. Using every minute of the day is important. What are you doing in your spare time? Watching TV? Playing games? Are you willing to give up these activities or at least cut back on them? Do you want to achieve your goals? Then work on them. If you have five minutes, put this time to good use. Read, do research, or act on your goals; do something. Make every minute count.

Lessons Learned

This chapter covered everything you need to know about how to achieve your goals. Implementing these concepts into your lifestyle is the hardest part. I asked the question at the beginning of the book, "What are you willing to give up to achieve your goals?" Once you have decided that your goals are important, you will be on your way to reaching them. During my life, I have applied the above concepts and other concepts at different times, in order to achieve my goals. There is no one set of rules or order that you must use these techniques to reach your goals, but you will use most of them at some point in your adventure.

Decide what you want in life and start putting together the plan on how you are going to achieve that goal. For those who do not have time to read, put the book by your desk, and before you go to lunch, read one page. Try to read one page a day. This gets you in the habit of reading and learning. Before you realize it, you will have finished the book and be on your way, but you must start.

What if you do not know what you want in life but simply want something better. Ask yourself this, if I won the lottery today what would I be doing? This is your dream or goal that you should be working toward. Another way to find your dream is to ask what your favorite hobby is and how can you turn that into a living. If this did not work, start out by setting small goals, such as going to a gym once a week, reading a book, or trying a new sport. You do not need to know your life purpose today. By trying different things in your life, you might find what you want to do. Reading this book and other books will help you to be aware of your surroundings and discover what you really want out of life.

Depending where you are in your life, this plan can take days, months, or even years to develop. This is not a short-term plan. Over the next few months and years, you will develop the techniques needed to succeed at anything you set your mind to. Your attitude will improve, and your results will be amazing.

Everything in life has consequences; nothing happens by accident. You control your own fate. The decisions you make are a cause and effect relationship; when you make good decisions, good things will happen. When you make bad decisions, bad things will happen. Sometimes people overlook the simple things, such as doing a good deed or simply saying good morning to someone. The more positive you are, the more people will respond to you positively.

If you go to work late one day, the result is usually not much; maybe your boss will tell you come in on time. But if you go in late repeatedly, your boss will finally have enough and fire you. You will blame your boss for letting you go, but in reality, it was our own doing. You cannot blame anyone else for what you do; you must take responsibility for your own actions.

Exercises

1. Where are you on Maslow's Hierarchy chart?
    By identifying your position on the chart, will provide a better understanding of what your priorities are going to be.
2. Start to think about what you want in life and what are you willing to give up to achieve it.

Notes

Chapter 2

Dreams

- *What were Your dreams as a child*
- *What did you do for fun*
- *Early childhood*

I was born into a middle-class family in Northern New Jersey. My parents were from Jersey City. I was born at the Medical Center in Jersey City but never lived there. My parents had moved into the suburbs right before I was born. I am the second child of four. My sister is the oldest, and I have two younger brothers.

We were a typical family growing up. Both parents worked and my grandmother lived with us. My grandmother cooked, cleaned, did laundry, and helped raise us. My siblings and I went to public

schools. We all got through our early years and teenage years without many incidents or problems. My mother worked and later owned a travel agency, which allowed
 us to take annual vacations. They were nothing extravagant, but we had fun.

My sister was (and still is) very outgoing. When we were growing up, my sister would speak for my brother who is two years younger than me, and me when we tried to speak. From what they told me (I do not remember the details), it was so bad that my parents did not understand my brother and me. My sister would interpret what we wanted. This led to my brother and me going for speech lessons so we could communicate with the world.

We were a typical family; we would fight all the time, but we were well behaved. My brother and I were less than two years apart in age. We were typical boys growing up. We would do many things together. This led to us sharing our toys. Because of this, we got into many fights while growing up. Some of those fights ended in one of us getting hurt. Between the both of us, we had received stitches and more than one broken nose.

One of my first memories was doing something mischievous. My parents would make my brother and me walk to church and religious education classes every Sunday. It was not far—about a mile from home. My parent's plan was that we would attend mass and then go to religious education. We did this most of the time. Then one day neither of us wanted to go to church, but my parents insisted. We had a revelation that no one really knew if we attended church or our classes. Therefore, from that day on we would walk to church but not attend either one. We would get the church bulletin and hang out. Later when we arrived home, we handed my parents the bulletin. They assumed we went to church and the religious education class. In reality, we were in the backyard, hiding behind our shed. In the winter, it would get cold, so we started a small fire to keep warm. Having a fire in the backyard was not one of our best ideas because someone in the house saw the smoke and caught us. Then we had to go to church and religious education until we made our confirmation.

In fifth grade, I had my first operation due to appendicitis. I do not remember much, but I do remember being doubled over in pain one day after school. I was riding my bicycle on the street and just felt a pain in my side. I fell to the pavement and my brother got help. The next thing I knew I was at the hospital getting ready to have my appendix removed. The recovery was not bad—plenty of ice cream and watermelon.

Middle school was nothing special; I attended classes and passed all of them. School was not that important to me, but I had to go. I was not involved in any sports during middle school. I did try out for track one year, but it was a lot of work and running. Over the entire season, I never won a race. One race I came in third. OK, there were only three of us racing, but I got some points. The two sports I showed interest in were riding motorcycles and skiing.

One of my friends had a minibike that I rode, and I had a lot of fun. It was small, but we had fun riding it in his backyard. My first motorcycle was a gift from my parents: a Honda CT70—a small semi-automatic motorcycle for my brother and me to use. This meant we still shifted, but there was no clutch to squeeze. My brother and I were supposed to share the motorcycle, which we did some of the time. I monopolized the motorcycle, and my brother would use it when I was not on it. We would ride it in the backyard most of the time. My friends and I would go into the wooded area not far from our house and ride. Gas at the time was under a dollar a gallon. For a few dollars, we would ride from sunrise to sunset, rain or shine, summer and winter. That was the beginning of my riding career.

My middle school had a ski program available to the students, with ski trips to local resorts after school. Even though I did not know how to ski, I signed up because it looked fun and was something I really wanted to do. The bus would leave right after school, returning at around 11:00 p.m. I went with thirty to fifty other students I did not know—not caring that none of my friends wanted to go. I wanted to ski, so I went on the trip.

I spent my first day more on the snow than on skiing; however, I loved it. It was cold, and gliding on the snow was great. I remember skiing at night and being on the slopes with just the lights and no one around me; it was so peaceful. I fell in love with skiing for this reason. I went on ski trips every week during that first season and was actually able to ski down the mountain without falling. Over the next few years, most of my friends started skiing.

"We learn by doing things rather than talking about them."
St Paul

To support the sports that I loved, I had to get a job and make money. There are not many jobs available to fourteen-year-olds. I finally got a job delivering newspapers after school and on the weekends. The route was small during the week, about fifty houses and on the weekend, seventy-five houses. I would get home from school, pick up the papers at the leader's house, and then deliver the papers. By working, I was able to have money to enjoy skiing and riding. This paper route required me to deliver the papers seven days a week no matter what the weather. During the summer months, it was not bad. However, during the cold months being on a bicycle in the rain or snow was not pleasant. But, it was a paycheck.

A year later, I was able to find a job working as a dishwasher at the local restaurant. For the most part, I put dishes and other stuff in a dishwasher and then emptied it out. I also kept the shelves stocked with food items. The working age was sixteen, but they never checked my working papers, so at the age of fifteen, they hired me. I worked mostly weekends and occasionally a night during the week. I stayed a few years and became a waiter. The job was fun and I was making money.

I hated high school and was fortunate I only had to spend three years there. This was because ninth grade was in the middle school. The year I graduated from middle school was the last year it included ninth grade. Therefore, my class of incoming sophomores moved into the high school at the same time the grade behind me moved up as freshman. This made the transition much easier because we were not the youngest class in high school.

My high-school experience was nothing special. I do not remember many of the teachers there or what they taught me, but literature was a class I remember liking. We read mostly science-fiction books and short stories. The stories were great, but the passion the teacher had is what made the class so much fun. I think it was the only class during high school I enjoyed and never missed. Other than that class, I did not care about school. Once in high school, I did just enough to pass, as I had other things to do. I would study enough in order to pass. I would fail some tests and not hand in papers, but I would get a one hundred on a paper or test when I needed it. I was not motivated to do anything in school. I did not participate in sports or other activities in high school, I just wanted to get out as fast as I could.

     I figured out a way to not go to school and still get my diploma: get a job. My junior and senior years I was in the work-study program. I would attend classes in the morning then go to work in the afternoon. I thought this was the greatest thing ever. I did not think what I was learning in school was worth anything. Instead, the school graded me on how I performed at my job. My supervisors had to fill out reports on my work. That was an easy A because I enjoyed working. In addition, working allowed me to earn money to support my skiing and motorcycle hobbies.

During my first year in the work-study program, I worked for my parents. They owned a travel agency, and I worked a half day in the afternoons for them. I filed papers, delivered tickets to clients, and answered phones. My transportation at that time was a moped, my first on-the-road motorcycle. I remember walking into the store with $400 and paying cash for a moped. I drove it home that day. That was my primary mode of transportation until I got my license.

My senior year in the work-study program, I decide to work in a tool and die shop. I started by sweeping the floors and taking out the garbage. I guess I did a good job because they hired me full time after I graduated high school. I was working with my hands and mind, and learning a trade; this was a perfect job for me. The job consisted of making stuff that people could buy. I remember going to a store and seeing one of the things I made for sale. I had a great feeling of pride, thinking that I made that item.

At the time, I thought I did not need more schooling, that I did not learn anything in high school. What could college teach me? I was working, making money, and having fun. I was able to buy toys and go on vacation. Many of my friends were in college studying, but I was making money.

Learning is not compulsory...neither is survival."
W. Edwards Deming

When I was young, I would watch my father fix things that had broken around the house. His philosophy was if it was already broken, what was the worst we could do, break it some more? If needed, he would call a technician; otherwise, we fixed it and saved some money. I used this method to learn about repairing different items. I started repairing my bicycles and motorcycles. They broke a lot, and I never had the money to pay a shop to do the repair. Therefore, I learned how to fix simple things. I carried this philosophy into working on cars. I had limited income and wanted to spend that money on riding and skiing, not on doing repairs.

I did not know much about cars, but I was somewhat mechanically inclined. If there was a problem with a car, my friends and I would take it apart and figure out what was wrong. Between all of us, we did everything that a person could do on a car. At one point, a friend and I started doing simple tune-ups and oil changes for extra money. We did a few complete engine rebuilds. We had fun and made some money at the same time. I found another way to make money doing something I loved.

My parents bought a vacation home in the Poconos in Pennsylvania. I use the term home lightly; it was literally four walls and half of a roof. I do not know what they paid for it, but I remember them saying their car cost more than the house. They had a contractor come in and finish the walls and roof. They could then at least consider it shelter. As a family, we would travel up there on the weekends and work on making repairs. For the most part, none of us knew much about building a house, but we learned by doing. We made many mistakes, but we just kept building. We did just about everything in the house. The work that we did never looked professional, but it was reasonably good. It took several years of many weekends, but in the end, we had a vacation home that we could enjoy. My friends and I would use it when we went skiing nearby.

Lessons Learned

When I was growing up there was not much I wanted or worried about. My parents took care of everything. I simply had fun, went to school, and started working at a young age. I understood the value of money. My parents never pushed me or my brothers and sister to do anything; at that time sports were not as big as they are now. I floated through my childhood with no drama. Now that I look back at some of the things I did when I was young they were for fun. My goal was simply to have fun. I had a few jobs to pay for motorcycling and skiing.

I learned at a young age that if I wanted to have fun I needed money. I did not like working, but I liked playing, and I needed money to play. Working was a means to an end; I wanted to do things and buy stuff.

My parents taught me to take some chances, like fixing something that was broken. I learned to work on houses, cars, bikes, and motorcycles because I could not afford to pay someone to fix them. The same thing my parents did with their house. We did all the work to save money; this is called "sweat equity."

My primary schooling was also typical. I did not like school, but it came easy as long as I applied myself, which was not that much. During high school, I learned how much I hated school and wanted nothing to do with it. During that time, I never understood what or why we were learning. To me it was applicable to what I needed to get by in life. I would miss classes when I thought I could get away with it. I passed all my classes with the least amount of effort.

After graduating from high school, I was able to work full time. I understood that if I traded time for money (working), I could afford to buy things. The first major purchase of my young life was my moped. I had saved for it for a few months and shopped around until I found the perfect one at the right price. Not only was I proud that I bought it all on my own, it also provided me a means to get around. You would be surprised how far you can get on a 49cc moped, which got 70 mpg. It was freedom for a fifteen-year-old.

Attitude—My attitude at the time was to have fun and enjoy life—I was a teenager. As a teenager, I thought I knew everything. I had no thoughts on how I should think or why. I wanted to have fun and that was all. I did not look for the best in a bad situation. I simply lived life like a teenager, wanted everything "now," and did not really care about anything else.

Desire—My desire at the time was skiing, riding, and having fun. I did not have a burning desire for much of anything. If for some reason I could not go skiing, no big deal...maybe next time. If I failed a test at school, no big deal, I might do better next time. I had a very easy personality, I did not want to stress.

Faith—What made me get on a bus and go skiing that day? I did not know anyone on the bus nor did I even know how to ski. I am glad I got on the bus to learn to ski. I look back and realize I had the desire to learn to ski. For me, it was a major step to do something totally by myself without any friends to support me.

Knowledge—I was going to school, which I thought was a waste of time, but I did graduate. My method of learning was hands on. I liked taking things apart to see how they worked and gained my knowledge through doing.

Maslow's Hierarchy—During this time of my life, I was young and did not think much of anything. My parents provided me the first three stages of the need's chart. I had biological, safety, and love needs taken care of. I could live and have fun; I was not worrying about surviving.

Planning—I got a job delivering newspapers to earn money. But the real reason for the job was so I could ski and ride motorcycles. That was my first lesson in planning. I wanted to do something, so I put a plan together to earn money to pay for my hobbies. The plan was not complicated or involved: earn money to ski and ride.

Reward system – My two hobbies provided me an outlet. Some teenagers don't have much stress, but at the time, they believe the world is against them. Escaping into my hobbies allowed me to have fun and remove any stress. These two items were my reward system. I was a teenager; I could spend all my money on fun stuff, no bills to worry about.

Success through failure—I learned to work on bikes, cars, and other things, because I did not want to spend money on getting things repaired. I failed many times at repairing things. I would just take something apart and start over until I got it right. Working on my parent's house, we made many mistakes, but we finished it, and it was livable.

Time Management—During this part of my life, time management was not much of an issue; my parents told me what to do: go to school and do homework. However, on the weekends—again, not that difficult—I would go out at sunrise, play, and return when it got dark.

Exercises

1. Review what were your major accomplishments in your life, and how did you achieve them.
   Review this to keep you motivated.
2. Look back at your life and identify your strengths and weaknesses.
   This will provide areas that you will need to work on to achieve your goals.
3. What hobbies did you have as a child, are you still doing any of them? Start looking for a hobby.
   Provides an escape from work.

Notes

Chapter 3

Faith / Attitude

- *Early Adult*

I graduated high school on Friday, and on Monday I was working a full-time job as a tool and die maker. I was working forty-plus hours a week making great money (for someone just out of high school). I had money to spend on the things I wanted to do, ski, ride, and have nice cars. I thought I knew better than most of my friends that went to college. They were busy studying and never had money. I had a full time job, a trade I was learning, and did not have to go school. I thought I had the world at my feet. I could enjoy myself while my friends were wasting their time in college.

Over the next few years, I would learn a trade working with my hands. The tool and die industry is very labor intensive. There is a physical demand required to move the heavy plates. The work can be dangerous at times. Working in any manufacturing industry is hazardous.

I had a freak accident while working there. I was working on a lathe, cutting some steel down to size when a piece of metal flew up and got behind my safety goggles, landing in my eye. It was extremely painful. I remember wearing an eye patch for a few days. Luckily, this had no effect on my vision. The only issue was when I got contacts; I had to get a pair that went over the scar.

During the winter when I was not working, I skied as much as possible. My brother Jerry and I joined a local ski club, and we would ski four to five times a week. We would ski locally during the week. Skiing at night locally was usually within an hour of our home. On the weekends, we would head to Vermont for the day. We would leave at four in the morning, get to the ski resort by eight, ski all day, and drive home that evening.

One ski trip to Whiteface Mountain in New York State, my friend and I left at four in the morning and arrived at eight in the morning. We were the first ones on the mountain. We got on the lift, and at the top of the mountain, we headed away from the people in front of us to find an un-skied trail. As we dropped into the trail, I was on the right side and made the first few turns. I did not see the snowmaking pipe in the ground. My ski tip caught the pipe causing me to flip over. I stood up and felt OK. I started skiing, and everything was good until I attempted a turn to the left. My right knee just gave out. The ski patrol came and took me off the mountain in a sled. It was the most uncomfortable ride I ever had going down a mountain. After an hour in the first-aid station, they wanted me to go to the hospital. Instead, we drove home. My friend did ski down the mountain, but I never completed one run.

I went to the hospital, but they could not do much because of the swelling. I went to a doctor and he determined it was a soft-tissue injury. At that time, there was no such thing as an MRI, so the doctor had to inject me with a dye that would attach itself to the soft tissue so he could see it in the x-ray. This hurt just as much as the initial injury. The result was a torn meniscus, which ended up lodging in the joint. I had surgery to repair my knee. The good thing was this happened at the end of season, and I would not miss much skiing that year. Also, riding season had not yet started, so I would have time to heal and be ready to ride in the summer.

One more ski adventure I had is worth mentioning. A group of us went skiing at a local ski resort in New York. We were having a great time. As many teenagers do, we would race down the mountain to see who could get to the bottom first. This day was no exception. As we were heading down the mountain, my brother and friend hit each other. This sent my brother sliding down the mountain. At the bottom was a snowmaking gun. He hit his back on the snowmaking gun and was in a lot of pain. The ski patrol came and took him to the first-aid center. They could not do much for him and recommended he head over to the hospital. They then proceeded to tell us that the ambulance ride would be $500 cash. We were teenagers and did not have that kind of money. Our solution was to put my brother, while on a backboard, in the back of my hatchback car. To fit him in, we put the passenger seat all the way forward. I then drove him to the hospital. My brother had x-rays done and was diagnosed with no broken bones or other serious injuries—he was just banged up. He was able to sit in the car normally for the ride home and was very sore the next day.

"Do what you can, with what you have, with where you are."
Theodore Roosevelt

A few years later, my brother and I decided to open a tanning studio. We did some research and started looking for a location. We found a great location with three colleges near by. We leased a store and renovated the office space to fit the needs of the tanning studio. My brother worked at the studio during the day. I worked at night, and we split the weekends. During the winter months, the place was booked solid; the summer months we would just survive. We had the business running for about two years. This was the beginning of working multiple jobs in my life. The studio was fun, but we did not make much money at it. Then the property owner wanted to double our rent. We were not making enough money to support that kind of increase. After two years of having the business, we decided to close the tanning studio.

I was getting tired of working hard at the tool and die shop and not getting anywhere. I decided to go to school. I was still not ready for college so I went to Computer Processing Institute where I learned about computers. This was the beginning of attending school at night. I would go to work during the days, go to school four nights a week, and have fun on the weekends. I went for twelve months and came out with a certificate as a computer technician. I never thought school could be fun, and it taught me basic information about computers.

I was able to find a job in the electronic field. I built electronic equipment and put together circuit boards and power supplies. At this time, the computer field was still a relatively new field. Home computers were still not widely accepted as they are today. But after a few months of working, I had learned everything and there was nothing new. The work was very repetitive and boring; it was a little assembly line. It was technically challenging but not what I liked. I enjoyed making things and working with my hands and mind.

An opening became available in the quality department as an inspector. I was friends with the manager, and because of my tool and die background, they hired me. I was doing inspections of all incoming parts, final assembly, and work in progress. The job was much more enjoyable; I was moving around and never experienced the same thing twice. There were also new problems to resolve daily. I was using many of the same techniques in the quality field that I learned as tool and die maker. The most important thing for me was that I was thinking again. Little did I know this job would lead me to working in the quality field for the next fifteen years.

"Creative minds always have been able to survive any kind of bad training."
St. Bernard

After a few years, it was time for a new job. At my current company, there was no room for improvement or growth. I was able to find a job at a machine shop. I was going to be a quality inspector.

It was at a small family-owned company. The inspection department was small—about eight employees working over two shifts. I would be on the first shift, verifying and inspecting manufactured parts. I was working as much as I could, even a few double shifts. After some time, I received a promotion to supervisor. It took a lot of hard work and long hours to achieve that promotion. I was the youngest supervisor the company had.

One of the more memorable experiences that occurred during my young adulthood was the death of my grandmother. It was not because we were close but because it was the first time I had to deal with death. My grandparents had a house by the New Jersey shore. This translated into a place for my friends and me to stay and eat free while enjoying the sun during the summer. The house was about twenty minutes from the ocean and the boardwalk. My friends and I would stay a few days each year. This was a good thing for kids that did not have a lot of money. Being a typical grandmother, she would make us breakfast before we left in the morning, and when we came back at night, dinner would be waiting. While visiting we would also help my grandparents around the house, fixing and painting things as a thank you for letting us stay with them.

Years later, my grandmother was diagnosed with cancer. She was in and out of the hospital for a few months. My family would go and visit, and it was never pleasant to see her in that condition. Then one summer day, my parents called and said I should drive down the shore and visit my grandmother. It was late at night; I think I arrived at the hospital around 9:00 p.m. When I walked in the nurse sent me out telling me visiting hours were over. I drove to my grandparent's house. My mother was there and told me to go back and tell the nurse that my grandmother was dying. This time they let me stay and see my grandmother.

I walked into the room and my father was there sitting next to my grandmother. My father and I were talking to her for about an hour. She was not responsive, but we talked to her anyway. Then she took a big gasp of air and stopped breathing. I was in shock. I ran out to the nurse's station and the nurse came into the room. The nurse tried to find a pulse and listened for a heartbeat. It was not there. She then looked at her watch, wrote down the time, and pulled the covers over my grandmother's head. I asked if she was going to do anything, but before she left the room, the nurse's response was simply, "she is resting now." My father and I remained in the room a little while longer and then left. The next few days the family completed all the funeral arrangements.

Lesson Learned

As a teenager, I was young, stupid, and thought I knew everything—the typical teenager. I thought I knew better than the people that told me to go to school. I was happy that I did not have to go to school anymore. I had a full time job and worked at a trade; I thought I was set for life. But over time, I became disenchanted with working so hard. I needed to do something better and didn't want to work so hard. I was starting to think about my future, something I had never done before. What did I want to do when I grew up, besides be rich and just play all the time?

Not having an education limited my choices to what jobs I could get. I wanted to switch jobs and found out that no one would hire me because I did not have a degree. I was not happy and was in shock. I did not want to go back to school. But I had to gain knowledge in order to have more job opportunities. Being resourceful, I attended a trade school and earned a certificate in computers.

I was able to get a job in an entry-level position in the computer field, which turned out to be extremely boring. After a few years in the computer industry, I switched to the quality field. I enjoyed this much more, and it was better suited for me. I was working with my mind and hands at the same time.

My brother and I opened a tanning studio. It was a fun adventure, but we really did not know what we were doing. We fumbled along, and after a few years, we shut it down for several reasons. For the most part, we had a good time. The small risk we took enabled me to learn how to run a small business and make money at it.

After hurting my knee from a skiing accident, I remember someone asking me if I would stop skiing because of the injury. I did not understand the question. Why would someone quit something they loved just because of a small injury? To me it was the same thing as if someone got hurt in a car accident. Would they stop driving a car? I learned at this point, people are going to try to talk you out of doing things that you want to do. If you believe in what you are doing, stick with it and enjoy it. Do not let anyone steal your dreams.

The death of my grandmother was a reality check. Being in the room when she died and having the nurse pull the blanket over her head was tough and sobering. This made me think that life is short and we should do what we love; we are all going to die one day. Live your life now.

Attitude—For the first time that I can remember, I had a positive attitude. I needed knee surgery and thought it was OK because it happened at the end of ski season and before riding season. I knew I would be OK, and this would not slow me down.

Desire—My brother and I had the desire to open a business. We knew nothing about running a business, but we wanted to succeed. We did the research on the laws and on the best equipment. We made mistakes, but we ran a successful business for two years. We simply would not let it fail.

Faith—When my grandmother passed away, it was my faith that led me to believe she went to some place better than the world we were in.

Knowledge—During this time of my life, I gained two types of knowledge. The first, I went to school to learn about computers. With this knowledge, I was able to find a job and make a living. The second was the tanning studio. My brother and I had no idea how to run a business but we learned. We learned how to deal with people, employees, and customers. Not everything we did was successful, but the overall business succeeded.

Maslow's hierarchy—I was still young and living at home. My basic three needs on the need's chart had been meet. But I had no real desire for, nor understanding of the next needs for achievement—I was happy and having fun.

Planning—I was still doing short-term planning and needed to have whatever I wanted right then. I did not want to wait for anything.

Reward system—At this point, everything I did was a reward system. If I wanted something, I bought it. This is not the meaning of the reward system, but I was young.

Success through failure—I switched jobs during this time frame. I learned something new but after a while found it to be monotonous. I could not do the same thing day in and day out. I needed to get out of that job. I was fortunate to find another job within the same company, a job that I enjoyed.

Time management—My time management skills were starting to take effect. I was working two jobs. I had to make sure someone was also working at the tanning studio. I was still trying to ski during the winter, but it was also the busy season at the tanning studio, so for the first time, I had to give up doing something for work.

Exercises

1. Work on believing in yourself and believing in your faith.
   > *Believe you can achieve your goals, refer to your list of accomplishments.*
2. Work on improving your attitude. You need to start seeing the good in everything. Read and think positive thoughts and actions.
   > *Act positive all the time and it will become the norm.*

Notes

Chapter 4

Planning

- *Meeting*
- *Dating*
- *Engaged to Lori*

I was a young adult working a full-time job. I dated a few girls after high school. One summer in my early twenties, I had just broken up with a girl I had been dating for a few months. My sister wanted to set me up on a blind date. I was open to the idea and had nothing to lose. I resisted a little. However, I eventually called Lori. I later found out it was a blind date for me, but not for Lori. Lori had seen me at my sister's wedding a few years earlier.

For the first date, I picked Lori up at her house. It was a nice cool night in the beginning of October 1986. The plan was to go a local restaurant for something to eat. If that went well we would go out for drinks. The dinner went well, and as with many women, I do not recall Lori eating a whole lot. After a pleasant dinner, we went to a piano bar for a quiet drink. We stayed a few hours and talked. We walked out to the car, and it was misting out. As I walked Lori to the car and opened her door, I gave her a kiss.

Over the next few months, we went out on a few more dates. On the first date, she gave me her phone number. About a month later, I found out she had a private phone. I guess after a month it was getting serious—she gave me her private number. The holidays were approaching, and we were still dating; things were going good. She admits that over the next few weeks she began to become fond of me.

During the short time Lori and I were dating, the topic of getting married might have come up once or twice in passing. I decided after four months to ask her to marry me. I bought the ring at a local jeweler. The night I decided to propose was in February. I told

Lori that I had to deliver airline tickets for my mother. We pulled into a parking lot that overlooked New York City. While sitting in my car, I gave her the ring and asked if she would marry me. It seemed like forever before she actually said yes; I think it took a few minutes before it registered.

We went home to see my parents. They already knew I was going to propose to Lori but wanted to see us after the big event. My parents were very excited by the news. Then we went to Lori's parents. They were not as excited as my parents were. We set the wedding date for the following November, nine months from our engagement and thirteen months after our first date. My parents were fine with the situation; Lori's parents were not so thrilled. However, both parents supported us and helped.

We were young and naïve. We did not want to live in an apartment, so we figured out what our income would be and started looking for a house. After all, you could never lose money in the housing market. We started looking for a place to live. At the time we were looking there were bidding wars going on. Houses would sell the same day they listed and the houses were going for thousands more than the asking price. Our first thought was to buy the perfect house. That was what everyone else thought. If a house came on the market and was perfect, it sold within hours. It was getting very frustrating, so we switched our idea; we found a house that needed work.

We found a nice little two-bedroom ranch; it was perfect—about a half hour commute to work for both of us on a small piece of land. The main reason we were able to get the house was that it needed a lot of work. Dark paneling covered the walls and the previous owners smoked. The bathroom was old and the kitchen was falling apart. We bought the house and became homeowners.

The house needed a lot of work. I was able to use the knowledge from working on my parent's house to work on our house. I had about five months to transform this smoke-filled house into our newlywed suite. I worked every night and weekend for months, tearing out walls, ceilings, and carpeting. The house was in worse shape than I thought. At one point there were no interior walls, you could see all the rooms in the house just standing in the living room. We took down walls and gutted the entire kitchen and bathroom. We were fortunate because my aunt and uncle just remodeled their kitchen, so we took the old kitchen cabinets. They were in much better shape than what was in the house. The hard part was trying to get them to fit into our space. It took a lot of work, cutting, and trimming but we were successful and had a new kitchen. We finished the house just in time for the wedding, with only a few minor things to complete; at least we were able to move in.

"A man builds a fine house; and now he has a master, and task for life; he is to furnish, watch, show it, and keep it in repair, the rest of his days."
Ralph Waldo Emerson

It was the summer of 1986, I was working my day job, working on our house seven days a week, and planning for a wedding. This is when I decided to go back to college. My thought process changed at this point; I was no longer looking out for myself, I now had to support a wife, house, and future family. I knew I had to do something where I could make more money.

I was working as many hours as I could at a manufacturing company as a quality lead—about fifty to sixty hours a week. A promotion opportunity came available. The quality engineer had just quit, and I was more than qualified for the position. I was already doing the work anyway. I applied for the position and waited. The company interviewed some other people. After a few weeks, I spoke to human resources, who told me they hired someone and that I had to train the new engineer. This did not sit well with me. Weeks passed and I spoke to a friend in HR on why I did not get the job. The answer was simple; I did not have a college degree. It did not matter that I had the knowledge and trained the person. This was the first time in my life I did not get what I felt I deserved. I worked hard and knew what the position needed. Because I did not have a piece of paper, I would not get a job. It did not seem right.

I had to do something. I was getting married and needed to support my wife and future family. How could I do this without a college degree? I signed up for a summer class at the local community college to see if I would like school. This was the start of my college career. I was nervous about attending college—was I smart enough to complete the classes?

I thought I might actually learn something useful that first class. I was nervous and excited at the same time. I was going to attend school one night a week. After all, I did not want to commit too much to something I was not 100 percent sure of. I picked up my books the week before and read them before class started. I went the weekend before to find out where the classroom was. I was ready for school, after being out of high school for six years.

When I showed up for class, I was one of the oldest students in the class. Most of the students looked like they were just out of high school. I was so much older; I owned a house and was about to get married. When the teacher started teaching and going over all the stuff we needed to do, I thought, I do not have time for this, I work full time and have stuff to do around the house. How am I going to do this homework? I left that first night of class wondering if this was for me.

I got home and wondered if I could continue with school. I had so much on my plate. How would I find the time? The next day at work was a bad day. I felt trapped, as though I had no other choices in life. I had no degree and no real talents. I decided I would finish my degree and get a better job. I signed up for two classes that fall.

We were done with the house less than a week before we married. During that long summer, Lori spent the time getting ready for the wedding and making most of the plans. I had input, but because she did such a great job, there was not a big need for me to make many choices. My big choice was which limo would pick us up. I went with the 1932 Packard.

On our wedding day, I woke up at 5:00 a.m. and helped my grandmother make over 1,000 pieces of pastry for the reception. She owned a bakery when she was younger, so she made our wedding cake as well. After perfecting the pastries, we delivered them to the hall. Next, it was time to get ready for the wedding. But first, I jumped into the hot tub, had a cigar, and relaxed a little. The Packard arrived to pick me up and drive my brother and me to the church. Lori arrived at 3:00 p.m., which was right on time.

The best part of the wedding was the beginning. I was standing on the alter waiting for Lori to walk up the aisle. Then the double doors opened in the back of the church and showed a silhouette of Lori standing in the doorway with the sun behind her. After the ceremony, we headed over to the reception. We had a typical reception for the Northeast—plenty of food and dancing. We had fun. The next morning we were on our way to California for a two-week honeymoon.

"A good marriage is one which allows for change and growth in the individuals and in the way they express their love."
Pearl Buck

We came home from our honeymoon and moved into our newly renovated house. It was perfect for us— not that far from work and in a nice area. We started the daily life of a married couple, going to work during the week and doing errands on the weekend. We had arrived into the middle class. We did not have a plan; we would see where life would take us. We were not thinking about kids or much of anything else. We did not go on any cool vacations. We owned a house, had a mortgage, and no extra money. I knew there had to be a better way to live, so

I started looking for ways to get rich. I read books on how to succeed. They all said about the same thing, sounded like a fraud, or wanted a big investment. At the time, Donald Trump was just starting to make a name for himself. I wrote him a letter, asking if I could work for him doing any kind of job, but never received a reply. Finally, I thought I had an answer, a method of changing the way I thought.

I found a book called *Think and Grow Rich*. This book was different from most of the other books I read. This book spelled out a plan that you could apply to life. The book implied many thoughts and theories that a person could use to succeed. To me the most important was no matter what you want in life you can achieve it. It was not about how to get rich but how to get what you wanted from life. I read the book and liked the concepts. However, I did not have the time or energy to put those concepts into practice. I still thought I knew better. I do believe this book planted a seed in my mind, which took awhile to develop.

Two of my friends were in similar situations. They also did not have any money. We decided to go into business together. Nothing big or chancy; we would do small jobs around others people's homes, such as painting and other odds and ends. Most of our clients were from word of mouth. The business was going well, and the work kept the three of us busy for a few weekends each month. It was extra money, we were having fun working together, and I was able to put into practice some of the things I learned from working on our house.

Lessons Learned

This was a busy time of my life, and it was the first time I felt like an adult. I had to put other people's needs in front of mine. I met my future wife on a blind date, got engaged, bought a house, got married, and started a small business. I was just trying to stay afloat by any means possible. I did not have an overall plan on what was going to happen next. I was going through life, letting life dictate what I was doing, and reacting. I made some first steps toward changes, but I was not in a position to take advantage of them.

When I met Lori, I knew quickly I wanted us to be together. The issue was convincing her of that. Lori's parents were not as thrilled as we were, but they were supportive. Lori and I bought a house, which needed a lot of work. We almost took the entire house apart and rebuilt it to make it livable. We were able to save a lot of money by doing most of the work myself. I used the skills to repair the house that I learned from helping my father. I also learned many new skills I needed to complete the remodeling.

I realized I needed a college education to work smart and make more money. I was accustomed to supporting myself and doing what I wanted when I wanted. For the first time in my life, I put someone else's needs before mine and enjoyed the feeling. Being married meant I had to change my thinking to include my wife. I started searching for a better way to survive; I reviewed many get rich schemes. I read the book *Think and Grow Rich*. This book provided the thought process of success. At this time in my life, I was not able to put it to use. However, the principals were sound, and this planted the seeds in my mind, which later would help me achieve my goals.

In the meantime, I started a small business with my friends doing simple repairs and painting. My friends and I had fun doing this while we earned extra money. We were able to put the skills I learned working on my house to use, help others, and got paid for it.

Attitude—I was on top of the world, I got married, bought a house, and started school. I was busy, but I was happy. I thought I could conquer the world.

Desire—I was married and had to think about supporting a family. I only wanted to provide for my wife, as this was my new priority. My desire was to survive, and I was doing whatever I could to do that.

Faith—During that time of my life, I had faith that I would marry and stay married. I also had the faith to get the house fixed and have it completed before the wedding. I knew I would finish my degree no matter how long it would take.

Knowledge—I had knowledge from working on the house in the Poconos to work on my own house. I also gained knowledge from attending school to earn a degree.

Maslow's Hierarchy—I no longer lived at home, was married, and had to support a family—everything changed. I was at the bottom of the chart. I had to make sure I could provide basic needs, such as food and shelter, not just for me but also for my family. This was a total shift in my thinking; I was no longer alone.

Planning—Still not my strong point, I was letting life dictate what I would do and when I would do it. I had started school, which I knew would take years to complete. This was one of the first long term plans that I had.

Reward system – We had no money; we sank every dime into the house. The rewards were a few days of skiing a year and an occasional bike ride. Getting married was my reward that year. I was living as an adult.

Success through failure—During this time of my life, I was working hard at my job—over sixty hours a week. I had the skills and knowledge but lost a promotion because I did not have a degree. I knew I would have to change this and started to attend school.

Time management—I found the time to work on the house, plan a wedding (Lori did most of it) and attend school. Somehow, I was getting everything done. I had to learn how to prioritize; I had to get the house completed. I was also going to school and getting ready for the wedding. I had no real free time to enjoy anything else.

Exercises

1. If you knew you could not fail, what would you do right now.

2. Create your plan for what you want to achieve.

    You need an understanding of what it will take to achieve your goals. The plan is a high-level, not detailed, look at what you need.

3. Work on determining what kind of knowledge you will need to reach your goals.

Notes

Chapter 5

Sacrifice

- *Moving to Connecticut*
- *Detailed plans*

Six months after my marriage, an opportunity came to me to work at a large organization, as I was not happy with the current company I was working for because of the promotion I had lost. The catch was the job was two states away. After discussing this with Lori, we decided I would take the new position. We would move to Connecticut. Lori would quit her job in New Jersey and find another one in Connecticut. It would not be an easy move; we owned a house, both of us were working, and I was attending college.

The company agreed to put me up in a hotel so we could sell our house, buy a new one, and then have Lori move up. While Lori was still living in New Jersey, I worked during the week and went home weekends. Friday night I would leave work at 5:00 p.m. and drive back to New Jersey. It took three hours, mainly due to rush hour. On the weekends, the same trip would take only an hour and a half. On Sunday nights, I drove back to the hotel. I did this for about three months.

Lori was wrapping things up in New Jersey. When she got a job in Connecticut, she moved up, and we both lived in the hotel room. The hotel was a single room with two beds and a refrigerator, which we paid an extra ten dollars for. We had to eat two meals out because we did not have a kitchen. At first, this sounded great, but it quickly got old. We also had to go to the Laundromat to clean our clothes. We stayed in the hotel about three months. In total, I spent six months living in a hotel.

Our house in New Jersey was not selling. The housing market had been rising for years and we figured we could get what we paid for it plus the cost of the renovation. I had always heard, invest in real estate—you cannot go wrong. We put the house on the market for what we bought it for plus what we invested in it, which turned out overpriced.

After about three months, we ran out of time. We put the house on the market to rent or sell. The company I worked for offered to buy the house. They made an offer, which at the time was very low, at about $15,000 less than what we had paid for it. This loss did not include the money we put into the house, so the real loss was over $25,000. We refused the offer. A short time later, we were able to rent the house, which covered the monthly expenses. We would have to deal with selling the house later, hoping the market would pick up.

"A hotel isn't a home, but it's better than being a house guest."
William Feather

On the plus side of the real estate market crash, we would be buying another house. The housing market in Connecticut was the same as in New Jersey. We had a large selection of houses to choose from. We found the house we wanted; it was a three-bedroom ranch a few blocks from Long Island Sound. In the winter when there were no leaves on the trees, we could see the water. The closing went through with no real issues. We were starting to settle into our new house, and at first, it was tough not having family or friends close by to help, but we adjusted quickly.

When we moved to Connecticut, I had to drop out of one of my two classes. The commute would be too long. There was no Internet at that time, so I had to show up for three classes: the first day, mid-term, and final. The rest of the classes aired on TV, and I had to mail in the assignment. I would record the classes and watch them on the weekends until I completed the work. I searched for a school to transfer my twelve county college credits to, and a college that had industrial engineering accepted me. The program sounded good, so I started to attend classes. The more classes I took the less I liked the program and the school. They had a campus, but very few classes were on campus; many were off campus at different companies throughout the area.

I switched to another school—Waterbury Technical College. They had a degree in quality assurance. I was in the quality field and thought this would be a perfect match. I have been working in the quality field for several years and this would allow me to learn more about the field. It was a two-year degree. I would start by attending class two to three nights a week.

Lori and I were settling in to our new home in Connecticut, both working full time. There was nothing special going on; we were just getting by, making our payments on the house and cars. In 1988, personal computers were still new. Not many people had them nor did many people even know what to do with them. I was using computers at work and liked working with them. I wanted one at home. I was using a typewriter for my school papers, and a computer would be much easier and faster to use.

We agreed we would get one. I started pricing them out. Damn they were expensive. The least expensive model was going to cost $2,000. That did not include a monitor or printer. The monitor and printer would cost an additional $1,000. We did not have the money. I was working and going to school at night, which did not leave much time to get a part-time job. One day while looking in the want-ad section of the paper, I found the perfect job—delivering newspapers in the morning before work. The pay for delivering the newspapers was about $125 a week.

I called up the company, had an interview, and got the job. The next week the supervisor met me at my house on Monday morning around 5:00 a.m. We folded the papers and stuffed them in the car. We headed to the neighborhood where I would be delivering the papers. He drove the car and threw papers out the window, all while following the list of addresses. There was no GPS at the time. I had seventy-five houses, and it took about an hour. The supervisor went out with me only one day before I was on my own. It was not that bad the first day, but it took about two hours to deliver the papers. I was getting better each day, and was never late to work.

Then when Sunday came, the number of houses jumped to 125. It took a few hours just to put the papers together. With my car loaded, I could not see out the back window. I was freaking out. I was supposed to be done by 8:00 a.m. everyday. That first Sunday I finished around 11:00 a.m. At least it was still the morning. Needless to say, I had many complaints about missing and late papers that day. As time went on, my time got faster.

Then winter arrived. It is 5:00 a.m. and about 10 degrees with all my windows wide open. I had the heat blasting, but it did not help—it was cold. The next day, I put on all my ski equipment, including goggles; I must have looked like an idiot. However, I was warm. The plan was to deliver papers in the morning, go to work, and then go to school.

It took me several months to save enough money to buy my computer. It had the latest technology, a 3.5-inch floppy drive, and a three-color monitor. It had a 10 MB hard drive. I took it home and booted it up, and there it was just glowing at the c:\ prompt, doing nothing. I could not afford any applications that took another few weeks to get. I purchased a word processing program, which I needed to write my papers for school. A few weeks later, I went all out and bought a printer. It was a 24-pin Near Letter Quality (NLQ) printer. At the time, 24 pin was the best available. The standard at the time was a nine-pin printer. I was now able to do my schoolwork more efficiently.

Lori and I had a plan to wait five years into our marriage to have children, as we could not afford to have them at the time. We were both working full time to pay for the house and other expenses. Then one day I came home and found Lori on the couch crying. When I asked what was wrong, she told me she was pregnant. I was happy and nervous at the same time.

So we had to change our plans. We started fixing up the house to have a child. Getting the bedroom painted, buying the baby furniture, and child proofing the house. The plan was for Lori to stay home with the baby for eight weeks on leave and then go back to work while the baby was in day care.

It was early on a Monday morning; my wife was tapping me on my head. As I opened my eyes, she said, "I think it is time." I knew what she meant and jumped out of bed. We got dressed and rushed to the hospital around 8:00 a.m. Three and a half hours later, we had a perfectly healthy baby boy, which made being away from family a bigger issue, as we had no one to help take care of him. We were on our own, though we appreciated Lori's mother spending a week and helping.

In the spring of 1990, I finished my associate degree in quality assurance. I celebrated and went to the graduation. I was working in the quality field and had determined to move up in the industry. At the time, an associate degree was the highest level I could get at any local college for quality. I belonged to a quality association, and in order to become a quality engineer I took a six-hour exam. It was much harder than I thought it would be, and I did not pass the test, which depressed me a little. I needed to study for the test because it was obvious I did not know everything. I read every book I could get on quality and passed the test the next time; I was a quality engineer. By studying for the test, I actually learned more about quality. I felt great that I had passed the test; I just had to convince a company I was as valuable as someone with a degree was.

"Everyone's a star and deserves the right to twinkle."
Marilyn Monroe

I was happy that I finished, but I was anxious to enroll at a four-year college in Connecticut and start working on my bachelor's degree in industrial engineering; this was the closest to the quality field.

It was time for Lori to go back to work, which meant our son was going to day care. Lori was not happy with this, but we had no choice. We spent a few months looking for a good day care center. We were not happy with any of them. We finally found one with a woman who was starting a day-care center in her home. She was state certified and was very nice. Our son received excellent attention, though Lori was not happy dropping him off; she would cry more than our son would. So, I started dropping him off in the morning and Lori would pick him up at night.

While attending school, a classmate approached me about making money. I had a new baby and needed to make money, so I went to his house for a meeting. The presenter talked about buying household products and getting other people to do the same. I thought I could do this and took Lori to a meeting, where we agreed to join Amway.

Amway's concept is to simply buy goods that you already use and get other people to buy them also. It is a lot harder than it sounds. I thought I knew a lot of people—how hard could this be? But in the end, none of our friends or family joined. I had to approach other people—strangers—and convince them to do this, but this was not my strength. Even though I believed in the concept, meeting new people was not my forte.

Amway has an excellent support system. They provide books, CDs, and meetings to help people accomplish the goals they set. Having that kind of support system helps people to continue and grow. One concept that I liked was dream building. This was going out and pretending to live the life you wanted. Go to open houses of a million dollar home, stop in a Porsche dealer and test-drive a car.

The two types of motivational meetings were local and regional. The local meetings consisted of local leaders motivating people through the success and motivational stories they had achieved. These meetings usually consist of 200 to 400 people.

The large meetings take place in football arenas, where thousands of people attend. The goal of these meetings is to motivate the masses—and they work. The meetings have dynamic speakers and include entertainment to help motivate the people.

Since I left Amway, the meetings are what I miss the most. Motivation is the key to success for Amway, and other companies should practice the same.

It was Christmas time, and after we put up all the decorations and were getting ready to celebrate the holidays, Lori said she was not feeling well and had been getting headaches. At one point, she could not even stand up for more than fifteen minutes at a time. She went to many doctors, but they could not find anything wrong with her. This went on for about four months. Out of desperation and the fact there were no other doctors we could see, Lori went to an allergist. It turns out she had severe allergies, and the Christmas tree triggered them. She received weekly shots and recovered quickly.

Life was going well; I was married, working a good job, going to school at night, and Lori was pregnant with our second child. I went to work one day, preparing to begin my normal work activities, when my manager called me into the office and laid me off. To say it was a surprise would be an understatement; it was a shock.

Lessons Learned

My goal at the time was short term; I wanted to be an engineer. I did not have the schooling or training for this job. I had the knowledge and I knew what to do, but I did not have the official paper work. I had an opportunity to get a step closer to becoming an engineer. It came at a cost of moving out of state to get a job that I thought would help me to achieve my goal. When an opportunity arises to help meet your goals, you must take it. I did not give up on getting my degree. One method to reaching my goal was taking long, so I found another way to achieve the same goal. School was my primary method, and accepting a job out of state was a second method.

You can lose money in the real estate market. We lost about $25,000 on the first house we purchased and sold because the market crashed. On a positive side, we were able to buy another house cheaper. Losing that much money was depressing, but I kept a positive attitude, knowing this happened for a reason. Not only did we lose the money we also lost all the value we put into fixing up the house.

Growing up others told us we could not lose money if we bought a house, and that it would only go up in value. The lesson learned was no one can predict the future, and just because something happened in the past does not mean it will happen in the future.

We were still newlyweds and I moved about two hours away leaving Lori for three months. When Lori joined me, we spent another three months living in a single hotel room. We went with the flow and did not fight the situation. We made the best of it, and, if anything, the separation made my heart grow fonder. I loved Lori even more than I thought possible. Living in one room in a hotel tested our patience for each other in such cramped quarters.

I had just started attending college after not believing in it. I knew the best way for me to stay connected to college was to continue going no matter how difficult it was. I knew that if I did not stay in class, the chance of me staying in school was slim. So I stayed in school. Attending college while in a different state did work and required more effort, but it was a great experience.

I really wanted a computer but could not afford one. I figured out a way to earn extra money—

delivering newspapers before work. Morning was the only time I had available because of school. Why did I want a computer? First, I would use it for school. It was something that was new and cool to have. I worked several months to save up enough money to buy the computer. This was the first time in my life I could remember using delayed gratification. It felt rewarding knowing that I worked hard for something and got what I wanted.

Like many young couples, Lori and I had a five-year plan. But that went out the window when Lori got pregnant with our son. Everything we had planned for needed to change. It was not ideal, but we knew we would make it work. Our priorities changed, and our focus was now raising our children. We changed our plan because we wanted to.

I was able to achieve one goal of becoming a quality engineer. It took many hours of studying and hard work. I had to take the test more than once to achieve my goal. One disappointment was it did not pay off as I thought it would. Most companies still wanted a college degree. But I was able to achieve the goal of becoming a quality engineer.

Attitude— During this stage of my life, I was going through many different attitude changes. When I was single, my attitude was one of distance and thinking I knew best; I did not want to hear from anyone. Then I fell in love and my attitude changed. I suddenly had to find ways to take care of and support a family. I was willing to listen and learn. For the first time in my life, I thought maybe I did not know everything. I was very happy but extremely nervous.

Desire—My desire was simply to provide for my family. I needed to get a degree so I could earn enough money to support my family.

Faith—Going through my layoff, I knew I would survive and find another job. While looking for another job none was out of the question; I even started to look at other cities. I had to provide for my family, and I knew God would guide me to the best position I needed at the time.

Knowledge—I got my first degree; I now know something about quality. I also gained knowledge through the training of Amway. It was completely different than what I went to school for. This knowledge was more about life and how to interact with people—how to have a better attitude.

Maslow's Hierarchy—I was moving up the needs chart; I had been providing the basic needs for my family. I wanted more in life; I was looking for achievements that I could make. I wanted more responsibility at work. Yes, I was still struggling to provide the basic needs for my family, but we were eating, had shelter, and had love.

Planning—My plans changed a lot during this time. When I was single, my plans consisted of where to go skiing and where to ride. I had no real plans; I was letting life decide what I would do next. However, once I got married, that changed. I had to think about another person. I wanted to be an engineer, so I went to school. I knew this was a long-term solution but I had no choice. I had an opportunity to take a step closer to my goal; I took a job 150 miles away to make that goal come true.

Reward system—I wanted a new computer, but we did not have the money, so I got a part time job to pay for it. It took several months to save enough money, but it was worth the investment.

Success through failure—I lost a promotion because I did not have a college degree. So, I attended college to get my degree. I lost a job at a time when we had a child and another on the way. I had to find a job quickly.

Time management—I was working three jobs and going to school. I had to make every minute count. I found a job that would not interfere with my life; I only had to get up an hour or so earlier in the morning. I did my homework during lunch and would read when stuck in traffic. (In Connecticut, there is a lot of very slow-moving traffic. I made every minute of the day count.)

Exercises

1. What are you willing to give up to achieve your goals?

    Everything requires a sacrifice.
2. Provide more details on the plan and create a backup plan. Remember your goals will not change, but your plan will keep changing.

Notes

Chapter 6

Alternative plan

- *Moving back to New Jersey*
- *Building you attitude*

I got home and told Lori that the company had laid me off. She was in shock. The next day I started looking for a new job. The idea was to stay in Connecticut and in our home. The job market in Connecticut was not that great, and not having a bachelor's degree made my job choices limited. I spent the next few weeks sending out resumes and looking in the newspapers for jobs. After a few months of searching for a new job in Connecticut, I expanded my search back into New Jersey. I found a new job a few miles from where my parents were living. It was at a small, family-run company.

I moved back to New Jersey, leaving Lori, nine months pregnant, and my one-year-old son in Connecticut. We put our house on the market to sell. Once again, the housing market was not good, but we had no choice. We put the house up for less than we paid for it. This was the second house we were going to lose money on. We started packing the house to get ready to move.

I started working as a quality inspector at the family-owned company. They did not put much stock in my certification as a quality engineer, but it was a job, which would help pay our bills.

I moved in with my parents, and Friday nights after work, I would head back to Connecticut to visit Lori and my son, where we spent most of the time packing the house. Sunday night I would head back to New Jersey. I did this for only a few months.

I left Connecticut late one Sunday night, got back to New Jersey after 11:00 p.m. and was just getting unpacked. Lori called and said, "I think I am in labor." We went back and forth for the next few hours, until she was sure it was going to happen. I went outside at 3:00 a.m. to get in the car. The car looked funny; it had a flat tire. I had to go inside and get the keys to my parent's car. As I started to drive, I noticed the fuel gauge was below a quarter tank. I hoped I would make it there. Not many gas stations were open at that time of night; however, I did make it to the hospital without running out of fuel.

Lori called friends to take her to the hospital, and I met her there with a half hour to spare. At 6:00 a.m. our daughter was born. I spent the next week in Connecticut. It was nice to be home with my family and taking care of my son. After a week, Lori's mother joined us and helped with the two kids. I went back to New Jersey and work, resuming my commute between the two states.

We could not sell the house in Connecticut, so we found someone to rent it on a monthly basis.

We thought we were set, but the people moved out after only two months. Lori and the kids had moved to New Jersey. We rented a three-bedroom house that was conveniently located between my work and our families. We were paying rent on the house we lived in and paying a mortgage on a house in Connecticut.

I had been attending the University of Bridgeport in Connecticut when I got the job in New

Jersey. I was in the industrial engineering program. I was not able to complete the classes, so I started looking for a different school to attend. Many schools offered what I was looking, and I chose Montclair University. They had the industrial engineering degree I was looking for, and they took all my credits from the other schools I attended. Montclair was only a forty-five minute ride from work and a half hour from home.

I was taking anywhere from one to three classes a semester. Then after about two years, I received a letter from Montclair stating that, due to low enrollment in the industrial program, they were going to discontinue it, and that I needed to talk to a counselor. When I met with the counselor we went over my options, but there were not many. The one option I ended up accepting was to enroll in the "management information system" program. Any other option would have resulted in the loss of credits and delayed my finish by years. The main reason I decided to pursue this degree was the school would accept most of my classes. I would still lose a few classes, which would extend my time in school less than a year. This was the best choice because the other programs would have added several years to my schooling, and I was getting tired of going. We were renting on a monthly basis because we still had our house for sale. Finally, we got the call we were waiting for; the house had a buyer. Once again, the offer was lower than we wanted, but at this point, we just wanted to get rid of the house. The price was less than we paid, even less than what we owed on it. We were not thrilled with the idea, but we wanted to move on with our lives.

  I contacted the bank and asked if we could get an unsecured loan. Their response was yes, and they sent out a package of paperwork for us to complete and send back. We followed up, and they told us they did not see any issues with the application and that everything was on schedule.

  The closing date was getting closer and we still had not received approval for the unsecured loan. We made phone calls and they told us not to worry—everything was fine. The day of the closing, there was still no approval from the bank. Our lawyer contacted the bank, and they told him they denied our loan; they would not give him a reason. The sale of our house was not going to be completed and we could not afford a mortgage and rent payment. We were at the lawyers office not sure of what to do; we were stuck with the house. Discussing this with the lawyer the decision was to file for bankruptcy. This would free us of the debt of the house. It would also ruin our credit score for the next seven years. Lori and I decided this was the best method for us at the time. Instead of walking out of the lawyer's office free of the house, we walked out in bankruptcy.

Several months passed and we had a court date to settle the bankruptcy. We went in front of the judge, who had all the paperwork and the reasons for filing. He asked if I had anything to add, and when he completed the paperwork, we were free of the house and the debt. Just like that, we were done with the house. We lost our deposit, five years of paying a mortgage, and our credit. But we were now able to get on with our lives and move ahead. It was a big relief getting rid of the house. This was the second time we had lost money in the house market. So far, we had lost about $80,000 buying houses high and selling low.

The company I was working for in New Jersey had a softball team. I am not the most athletic person, but I knew how to hit and throw a ball. I joined the team. It was fun. We were playing other companies in the area a few times week. Between games we would have practice. Most of the time I played center field, mainly because I could judge where the ball was going and run to catch it. At one game, our first baseman was not able to make the game, so I played first base. There is a lot more activity at first base than center field. The game was going well, and then the ball travelled just to my right. As I moved to get the ball, the second baseman yelled he had it. I turned to get back to first base, but my right leg caught in a small hole in the ground. My knee twisted, and I felt pain shoot up my leg. I did get back to first base for the out, but that was it; I could no longer walk on my right leg. My softball career as well as many other sports and exercise opportunities were over.

Back to the doctors—I had sprained the ligaments and torn cartilage. I had another knee surgery to remove the cartilage that was floating in my knee. I was on crutches for the next couple of weeks and then went on to rehabilitation.

Lori was home with the kids, and I was working to pay the bills and attending school. But we did not have enough money to make ends meet. Every month we were short on paying our basic bills. It did not make sense for Lori to go back to work. Her entire salary would go to day care. I found a job at a country club, working as waiter on weekends. Being a waiter was the only job available that would fit into my schedule.

The good thing about working at a country club is that the same guests come every month. This gave me a chance to get to know and serve them better. The club also hosted weddings. Serving 150 people at once was difficult, and the hours were longer. I worked mostly Friday nights and Saturdays. I would only work on Sunday if something special was going on. I remember a few weekends working a dinner service on Friday and four weddings over the weekend. The work was not bad and the tips were great. We were now at least able to pay most of our bills at the end of each month.

Then I had an opportunity to work as a repair person. A wealthy person from Wall Street needed someone to help around his house doing odd jobs.

The hours were extremely flexible, and the work was easy: painting and general repairs around the house. I was able to fit this in between my other jobs and school. If I did not want to do a job, I would ask for extra money, and he usually paid.

I remember that around the holidays he asked if I would come on Christmas Eve to assemble a ping-pong table. At first, I said no, but when he offered me too much money I could not refuse. The amount of money would pay for our Christmas that year, so it was worth the trip. I worked for them a few more months. I was now working a full-time job, working two part-time jobs, and going to school. I refused to give up school because this was the long-term plan to making more money.

"It is the working man who is the happy man. It is the idle man who is the miserable man."
Benjamin Franklin

Lori's mother had medical issues and was in a local hospital for observation and treatment. We went to visit her, and she looked good. She was in great spirits and the hospital was going to transfer her to a New York City hospital later that night for more testing. We were planning to go in that weekend to see her again, if she was still there. The doctors indicated that she would be home for the weekend. The phone rang at 2:00 a.m., which is never a good thing. A friend of the family told me Lori's mother had just passed away; she was only fifty-four. Something had gone wrong, and she passed away very quickly and unexpectedly. We spent the next several days on the wake and funeral. Everyone was in shock because it happened so fast and unexpectedly.

I was burning out working three jobs I did not want to do, going to school, and trying to find time to spend with the family; I needed a break. If I did not work three jobs, we could not afford to live in the house we were renting. We started looking for a smaller house, but could not find anything we liked. We finally decided to move to Pennsylvania.

My parents still had the small house in the local ski area we had fixed up as kids. It was a two bedroom, saltbox-style home. They were going to charge us minimal rent. This would give us a chance to save some money and allow me to work less. I went up on the weekend, fixed it up, and got it ready for us to live there full time. The house was originally built for only weekend stays. I had to paint, put in a bathtub, fix the deck, and build a shed. The house was extremely small, and we needed the shed to store essential items necessary to live. We also rented a storage unit and put everything in there that we absolutely did not need.

Lori and I packed all the small stuff in the house and moved up what we could. On moving day, we had movers pack up the remainder of our rental house in New Jersey and move us to Pennsylvania. The movers moved everything into the house that would fit, and then they started leaving stuff on the deck outside. It was getting late and dark, and there was no more room in the house. I remember walking outside after the movers left; it had just started snowing. A sinking feeling set in that not everything was going to fit in the house. There was more stuff outside than there was inside the house. There was no more room in the house. I just started bringing in the boxes, and they filled the house completely. The things we did not need on a day-to-day basis we put in the storage unit.

The commute to work was over an hour each way. The commute to school was over an hour and a half each way. The house was at the top of the mountain on a secluded road. That winter we had a lot of snow. I remember one storm left about eighteen inches of snow. It took a week before the county plowed our street. I had to take vacation time; work did not understand because they only had a few inches of snow.

I was busy at work; the company promoted me to lead supervisor and then to assistant manager. Then the manager left the company. At that point, I was filling in for him. We had people on three shifts. A manager that I worked for in the past told me it was important that I talk to all my direct reports as often as I could. This meant coming in to work before 7:00 a.m. and once again, I did not get the job because I did not have a degree. This was getting old very fast. I had my associate degree and was almost finished with my bachelors. I was doing the job, but because of a piece of paper, I could not get the promotion I deserved. I was disgusted and left the company.

I found another job as a quality supervisor at another company. I was excited, as it was an award-winning, quality manufacturing shop. I had ten people that reported to me across two shifts and three buildings. I was very busy. The first few months were good; I was learning about the business, learning how it operated, and meeting people.

After a few months, I was getting concerned about how they won the quality award. Their processes and documentation were not up to the standards that they should have been. As the months went by, I finally found out what happened. They had lied on the application to receive the award. I was devastated. I thought I made it to a good company that cared about their employees and customers, but I was mistaken.

It was also getting worse. The manufacturing manager that I reported to was asking me to sign off on product that did not meet specifications so that the number would look good for that week / month. When the customers received the product, they would call asking how I could let bad product out the door. I stayed at this company for about nine months; I could not lie to customers on a monthly basis. I started looking for another job. This was my last job in the quality field.

Because we lived in Pennsylvania, we were doing better financially, so it was time to move back to New Jersey. We started looking for a house to rent because we were still in bankruptcy and could not buy a home. We got lucky; my father-in-law had a house that he rented out, which became available. The people, who had lived there for over fifteen years, moved out at the same time we were looking. We got a slightly better deal than the people moving out did, but not nearly as good as we had in Pennsylvania. My father-in-law was happy it was not vacant, and we were happy it was affordable, close to work, and close to school. We painted the house and moved in. The kids were just starting school so it was a good time to move into an area that we thought we would stay for a while. We felt it was important not to move the kids around to different schools. We decided to send the kids to a Catholic School.

The school was small and they expected parents to do a lot of fundraising and helping out around the school to keep costs down. This was fine with us. Lori got a part time job at the school helping the preschool teachers.

One of the fundraisers at the school was a golf outing. It sounded fun. I had never played golf, but thought, how hard could it be? Hitting the ball into the hole sounds simple in theory; however, there is so much that goes into ball placement, the swing, the grass, the club, the weather, and the person's skill. I went to the driving range to practice before the fundraiser. It was not that hard to hit the ball from the artificial grass and have it go into the wide-open field. I was feeling good the day of the event. I got to the golf course, and the first thing I noticed was that the fairways were not as wide as the driving range. There were trees, ponds, and sand traps in the way; crap, this was going to be hard.

I was with friends that played golf, and my first tee shot went about twenty yards and into the edge of the woods. I was in for a long day. My golfing partners often moved ahead and waited for me at the green. I had fun and got my money's worth—hitting the ball a lot more than any other person. At the end of the day, we went to have lunch, and they were giving out awards for best golfer, lowest score, hole in one, and so on. We were sitting at our table not really paying attention, when I heard my name called. I had the highest score, and the award I got was the "most honest" player.

"Real integrity is doing the right thing, knowing that nobody's going to know whether you did it or not."
Oprah Winfrey

My next job was in the computer field. I was a UAT analyst. I remember coming home from the interview and Lori asked what my job title was. The next question was what it stood for. I had no idea, but the pay was good, and I was now going to be sitting behind a desk in an office. I finally found out what UAT stood for user acceptance testing. I was testing software with the users before it went into production; my job was to try to break the software. It was a great job and company. This was my first office job. It was one of the first jobs where I received a bonus. The company was new and growing; it looked like a great future.

I enjoyed this job. They paid for my education and allowed me to take off time to attend classes. Things were looking good both at work and at home. The people I worked with were all hard workers and friendly to be around. The director was helpful and took care of the people that reported to him. I actually enjoyed going to work. The company was growing fast. Then the company became big enough that another company bought it. Every employee in the entire company was let go over the next year. Being in IT, our group was the last to go. This was the second time I was out of work, but I had my degree.

I had graduated the year before the layoff. It took me fifteen years of going at night to get my bachelor's degree in management information systems. I did attend the ceremony with Lori and the kids. The ceremony was in an arena, which was nice. The only issue was the hockey team that called the arena home was going to the Stanley cup. That meant that the graduating class sat on the ice. They had put cardboard down over the ice, but it was cold. I was disappointed I did not walk across the stage, but it felt good to graduate. I was done with school.

I started looking for work again. I felt better having a degree that would open more doors for me.

But the economy was not that great and companies were not hiring. I kept looking for work, sending out resumes, and going on interviews. I finally got a job offer at a fortune 500 company. The downside was that it was a contract position, but I needed the work so I took the job. I do feel if I did not have the college degree, they would not have hired me for the position.

The contract at this large electronic company was for three months, with the possibility of renewal. The first three months flew by and they renewed my contract for six months. I stayed busy doing the assigned job. A few weeks before my contract ended I had not heard about it being renewed. I was starting to get nervous. I kept asking my manager, and the response was, "we are working on it, we need you, do not worry."

That did not sit well with me, so I started sending out resumes and went on a few interviews. It was the end of June—not the best time to find a job with summer coming and people taking vacation. The job market, at the time, was turning for the worse; jobs were not as easy to come by as in the previous years. I thought to myself, I should have taken a full-time job instead of a contract position. I had one interview the Tuesday of my last week. My contract was ending Friday, and I had no job. My thoughts were to enjoy the summer and continue to look for work.

That Friday morning I went to work, asked about my contract, and they officially told me that was my last day. I left work at around 4:00 p.m. not feeling good about losing my job and not having any means of making money. I was stressed most of the ride home, worried about how I was going to support my family. On the ride home, I got a phone call from the interview I had gone to on Tuesday. The person said I would have the job under one condition; I must be able to start on Monday. I replied that was not an issue, and I could start on Monday. I had a job by the time I got home, and Lori was just as surprised as I was.

My position was new to the company. The commute was about a half hour from home. The company had some nice benefits that I took advantage of. The IT department was small, with only about ten employees. We were the regional headquarters in the United States.

Lessons learned

This was a busy time in my life; my daughter was born, I had three different full-time jobs, had two different part-time jobs, lived in three different states, and completed my bachelor's degree. Through all of these, I was still trying to spend time with my family and help raise the kids. I knew no matter how bad things might have looked that we would survive; I would work and do anything to support my family.

The first layoff came as a total surprise. Lori was pregnant with my daughter, and our son was under two. This was a very stressful time in my life. I had no income, and no family or friends were close to help. I accepted a job two states away from my immediate family, but closer to my extended family. It was a difficult situation, but I had no choice but to make it work.

My schooling was not going as planned. My original goal was to be an industrial engineer; however, Montclair stopped offering this, so I had to switch to MIS. At the time, the only reason I agreed to this was to get it done. This changed all my plans on what I wanted to be when I grew up. I was able to find work in the computer field, and have made a living in it.

One of the hardest things I had to do was to declare bankruptcy. This was something I never thought I would do for many different reasons, but I was forced into this by the banks. The bank would not allow Lori and I to take an unsecured loan for the loss on the sale of the house. Even though in the long term, this was the best decision we could have made. My pride was hurt that I could not support my family. This brought the total loss on our houses to over $80,000.

Due to the bankruptcy, our credit was shot. I had two small kids and my wife was not working. This meant I had to get a part-time job. This was because I did not have a college degree, and not many companies were willing to take a chance on me. It meant I had to work harder for less pay. I was not making ends meet, so I had to get a few part-time jobs to support my family.

After a few years of working at this pace, I was getting tired and needed a change. We moved into a small two-bedroom house over an hour from work. Looking back at this now, I am not sure this was much better. I was not working as many jobs, but I was still away from my family.

Lori's mother had passed away unexpectedly. This was hard on Lori and her family. Lori handled this with great courage. The kids were too young to understand what had happened. I am sure Lori would have liked more time to mourn the death of her mother, but she did not have that opportunity while taking care of two young children.

For the third time, I lost a promotion because of not having a college degree. This made me want the degree even more. I found a new job with a company that had won a quality award, and I really thought it would be different. It did not take long to learn they did not earn the award. Then my manager asked me to lie to customers. I had a choice to make. Should I stay at a job that asked me to go against my integrity? No. I started looking for and found another job quickly.

I finally finished my college degree. It felt great and took about fifteen years from start to finish. I never gave up and accomplished a major goal. After graduation, the company I was working at got bought out, and the new leaders let just about the entire company go. I landed a job in a fortune 500 company. It felt rewarding to know my degree had paid off. I also started earning the money that I felt I deserved and had a job that I was qualified for.

Attitude—This time of my life was one of the busiest, and my attitude swung in different directions; however, it never got bad. It was not always as positive as I would have liked, but it was positive. I looked for the good in everything, and things usually turned out okay.

Desire—My desire was to make sure my wife and kids were cared for. I wanted to finish my degree and provide for my family.

Faith—God had to have a better plan for us; this could not be how he intended for us to live. At the time, we had no idea what the plans were, but we knew something better would happen.

Knowledge—I was still working on getting my bachelors degree. Even though I did not have a formal education, I had been working in the quality field for some time, and I had gained knowledge from working on the job. I even trained the people that I would have to report to. I did use the knowledge I learned to become a repair person and help pay the bills.

Maslow's Hierarchy—We went bankrupt, and I felt like we took several steps back on the needs chart. We were once homeowners and now were back to renting—still struggling to make ends meet. We moved out of state to save money. I was back to trying to provide basic needs for my family. I had no time to worry about achievements or moving ahead.

Planning—My plan was to earn a degree in industrial engineering. Once the school dropped that degree, I had to change plans. I ended up moving into the Management Information Systems field. This was not my original plan but it was still a degree.

Reward system—I do not think I had any rewards during this time. For the first time in years, I did not own a motorcycle or ski. I was working to provide basic needs for my family.

Success through failure—We filed for bankruptcy and moved to a house that was too small to hold all of our belongings. We had a choice to make: keep going or accept that we were beaten, and this was not an option. We spent a year living over an hour away from work in a house that is smaller than most living rooms.

Time management – While working a fifty-hour-a-week job, going to school at night, working as a waiter, and working as a repair person, I made every minute count. If I were sitting in traffic, eating lunch, or had down time between tables, I would read and write papers. I had no spare time.

Exercises

1. Be prepared if your plan fails or does not work.

    Plans sometime fails, create a second or third plan if needed. A failed plan does not mean a failed goal, it means a new plan.

2. Create a safe haven to work on your attitude.

    You will need a place to recharge, time for yourself to unwind. This can be a room, driving, or doing a hobby.

Notes

Chapter 7

Giving

- *Motorcycle*
- *Kidney*

I was working at a steady job, my family was doing well, and I felt like I had too much free time and was not being productive. After going to school for fifteen years, I missed not going. I had my degree and considered that I was playing on an even playing field in the workforce. I now needed to make myself stand out and be better than everyone else. Getting my masters would give me an edge in the workforce. I felt like I was not finished and still needed more schooling.

The company I was working for had an excellent tuition-reimbursement program. After looking at a few colleges and programs, I decided on an online school: the University of Phoenix (UOP). I really wanted the flexibility of the program and wanted to spend more time with my family. When I was going to school for my bachelors, it was very time consuming, and having to go to school was difficult. My children were getting older and we were doing more things as a family. The online school would allow me to attend school but still have the flexibility to participate in their lives.

The management information systems program would be eighteen months if I followed UOPs schedule. I chose not to follow it exactly and took the classes at a slower pace, taking over three years to complete the program. The program required a lot of reading and writing. I liked that the program was self-motivated. At the beginning of each class, I would get the syllabus for the entire class. This enabled me to work at my pace; if I had free time I could get ahead on some of the projects.

The group papers were difficult, and every class had them. Overall, it was a good idea and helped people to work in groups. However, sometimes I had groups that wanted to meet on the phone at least once a week. One group had people in time zones six hours apart. This made for many long night. In some cases, the call would start at midnight and last one to two hours, making for a short night's sleep.

During the time I was attending school, the town I lived in wanted to start a lacrosse team for kids. My son wanted to play. We attended the first meeting, which was very informative. One of the items that arose was the lack of coaches. Each team would ideally have a head coach and two assistant coaches. I volunteered to be an assistant coach. I had never played lacrosse and did not even know the fundamentals of the game, so I went to the bookstore and picked up several books. I worked with the head coach and began coaching the kids on how to play. It was a few nights a week and on the weekends.

Because I attended school online, I was able to go to every practice and every game during the season. I would simply do my homework and attend class later at night, during lunch, or early in the morning. The online school really enabled me to be a coach and not miss any games, or miss any classes.

I was even able to go on vacation any time of year and not worry about missing class because I would take my laptop. We would do the sites of the town and have fun all day. When we got back to the hotel, the kids would go to sleep and I would go down to the lobby, attend school, and do whatever work was required.

I graduated in 2004 with my masters from the University of Phoenix. Our plan was to attend the graduation in Phoenix, Arizona. We flew into Las Vegas, Nevada, and stayed there for a few days taking in the sites. We then drove the 300 miles to Phoenix (a boring trip), again, taking in the sites once there. My graduation was on Saturday morning. It was a nice ceremony.

I wanted to teach at the college level. I contacted the dean at Montclair, who was also my former teacher. I inquired about teaching and asked what I would need to do to become an adjunct at Montclair. I meet him for lunch one day and went over the requirements. He told me that, at that time, there were no openings and to contact him prior to the next semester. For the next three years, I contacted him at least twice a year about working as an adjunct teacher at Montclair.

In the winter of 2006, I received the email I was waiting for; an adjunct position opened, and I had my first class to teach. My first class was on the schedule, and I was excited about teaching. The class was on basic networking, and had eighteen students. I met with the dean to go over what he was expecting and any tips on teaching. I got the book, read it from cover to cover, took notes, and made slides to show to the class. The night of the class, I was so nervous; I had never spoken in front of that many people. The class went well; I had no major mistakes, but I did have a few minor ones. However, what I realized was that the students did not know I made any mistakes. Prior to every class that semester, I was so nervous. I completed the semester, and I am not sure if I had fun, but I did enjoy it. What I really enjoyed was meeting a former student of mine during the next semester. He told me that what I had taught him enabled him to get a promotion at work. This was the whole point of teaching—to make a difference in someone's life. It felt great helping others to reach their goals.

"If you have knowledge, let others light their candles with it."
Winston Churchill

It was time to buy a house again. Our bankruptcy had cleared off our credit report. One of the main concerns about buying a house was to keep the kids in the same school system. This limited our search to two towns. One town we simply could not afford to live in. I thought it would take days to find the house we wanted, but I was wrong—it took months. Lori prescreened many houses, and I would only look at the ones she liked. She looked at just about every house on the market we could afford, but did not find much we liked.

We found a house online, but when we went to look at it, it was off the market. Upon further research, we found out the house had not sold; the owner took it off the market. We found the listing agent and inquired about the house. He told us the family took it off the market but still wanted to sell it. We arranged for a tour of the house, and it was just what we wanted in the town we wanted. It was a three-bedroom ranch with extra rooms on a nice piece of land. The house would need a new roof, a new kitchen, and some minor work in the bathrooms. They put the house back on the market and accepted our bid. The commute to work would be a few minutes longer. Nevertheless, the kids would get to stay in the same school system.

We set the day of the closing, but it was the same date as our vacation. Lori and I were heading to Lake George for a motorcycle rally for a week, so that morning we packed the bike and headed to the lawyers office. The closing took longer than we wanted it to, but everything went smoothly and we were once again homeowners.

We came home from the motorcycle rally and started fixing up our new house—painting the rooms and cleaning the carpet. We had about a month to move out of the old house; therefore, we took our time and completed what had to be completed. It was looking good. I spent the next few weekends moving all the small stuff to the new house. We had movers come and move the big items. This move was much better than the one in Pennsylvania. We actually had space for everything. We were settling into the house that we owned, but the kids were not thrilled with the location because they could no longer walk to their friends' houses to hang out. We had to drive them.

My son was training for lacrosse and wanted to go for a run in a park near the house. I thought it would be fun to join him and get some exercise. We ran from the house to the park on the road—not too far–and started running around the lake. It was unpaved and had a mile-long path around it. About halfway around the lake, going up a slight hill, I stepped on a rock and twisted my ankle and knee. I stopped for a second, knowing that it was not good and that I had done some damage. I limped home. My knee was the size of a grapefruit. I put ice on it, but I knew something was wrong.

A few days later, I headed to the doctor's office because there was no improvement with my knee. I had an MRI on the knee and nothing definitive showed up, but I still had the same amount of pain and discomfort. The doctor also felt something was wrong; we set up an appointment for an operation. When he opened up my knee, he found the meniscal ligament disconnected from the bone. The doctor was able to correct the issue. This surgery was not as bad as the other two, and the recovery was much better. I was now on crutches for the third time and healing well.

While I was teaching at Montclair University, I realized that I wanted to switch careers. I had so many bad teachers that I felt I could do a better job. My new goal was to teach full time at the college level. I met with the dean again, and he told me I would need a doctorate degree. I did my research, and with the success I had at University of Phoenix, I applied for their doctorate program and they accepted me. My goal was to be finished in five years. If I followed the University's planning, it would take three and a half years to complete the program. I did not want to move at that pace. I still wanted to enjoy life and spend time with my family. The workload was much heavier than my master's program, with more reading and longer papers to write. I also would have to write a dissertation, and I hated writing. I would like to say that the next five years went on without any issues or obstacles, but that was not the case.

I was once again in school, working a full-time job plus teaching part time. I was getting busy again. The major difference between that time and a few years ago is that I really enjoyed the teaching. Yes, it was work, but I immensely enjoyed teaching people and watching them learn. Once again, time management was a big part of my day. I wrote papers whenever I had time at lunch, before school, after school, before work, or after work. There was one advantage to teaching while going to school; I was always on campus and had access to a library.

During the spring months, my motorcycle was my preferred mode of transportation (I would only take my car if I had to). A year after I started school again, I was on my way home from work, riding in heavy traffic. I was riding in the left lane of a four-lane highway; the traffic was moving between 0 and 20 mph. It was a beautiful May afternoon. I started to slow down because the car in front of me slowed down. All of a sudden, the motorcycle accelerated, and the front wheel rose about four feet in the air, and I hit the car in front of me. As the motorcycle fell to the left, I rolled off onto the ground into the median, hitting the center divider. I then realized I a car behind me had hit me from behind, which pushed me into the car in front of me.

I was wearing all the proper protective gear, but my hip hurt, so I was going to go to the hospital for x-rays. As we were waiting for the police to come, my head started to spin and I felt sick. I got in the ambulance and headed to the hospital. A few hours after the accident, the pain in my neck, shoulder, and hip started to sink in. I got all kinds of x-rays, and when doctors told me I would be in pain for a few days, they were right. The bike was totaled because the accident caused a lot of damage to the motorcycle.

My shoulder did not get better over time. As the days passed, I could not lift my arm or move my shoulder much. In addition to the pain in my shoulder, I was losing feeling in my entire arm. The x-rays showed nothing broken, which was good. I needed to get an MRI of my neck and shoulder. The results indicated that I had a torn rotator cuff and needed surgery to repair the damage. The doctor felt this would also relieve the pain and numbness in my arm.

The recovery time would be six to eight weeks. This was an issue because I had been planning to take a motorcycle trip with several friends from work in a few weeks. The doctor thought that it would not get any worse, and we could postpone the surgery until after the trip. The motorcycle trip was a week of riding through five states, stopping at major Civil War battlefields. I scheduled my surgery for a few weeks after I would return from the trip.

Meanwhile, one day, Lori noticed the shower was leaking hot water, and we could not shut it off; it was becoming a sauna in our bathroom. After a few days, it finally got to the point that it was constantly running a stream of hot water and causing the mirrors to steam up. I had worked on houses, so I tore apart our main bathroom.

I had to replace the entire bathroom: the shower, walls, vanity, fixtures, and floor. While replacing the tile on the floor, I must have kneeled down hard on something. The next day my knee started to swell. At first, I thought I bruised it and figured the pain would go away.

That weekend I went to my parents' fiftieth-wedding anniversary party. After the party, I ended up going to the hospital, as I could not stand on my leg anymore. The doctors initially tried to drain my knee, thinking there was fluid in it. There was no fluid and they only drained blood. At that point, I wished I had not gone to the hospital.

After about an hour of them trying to drain liquid that did not exist, they called a specialist. He realized my knee was infected, and that there was no fluid in my knee. Somehow, I had damaged a small sac of liquid in my knee that provides lubrication. The sac had burst, caused my knee to swell, and caused extreme pain. They gave me antibiotics and admitted me into the hospital. I stayed several days until the swelling went down, and I could walk again with limited movement.

The following weekend I was to leave on the motorcycle trip. As long as I did not put pressure on the leg, I was fine and could ride. The riding part of the trip was fine, and I had no problems. However, a couple of the sites we stopped at required a lot of walking, which I did not do. I stayed close to the bikes while my friends walked around the battlefields. Between my knee and shoulder pain, I decided to cut the trip one day short. This turned out to be good. When I left, it was a beautiful day, and I made it back home with no problems. My friends stayed, and the next day it rained the entire ride home.

I got home from my trip and had the surgery on my shoulder. The doctor repaired the torn tendon and removed some bone spurs. The recovery was a few weeks of physical therapy. I did not realize how much I used my shoulder until I did not have access of it.

However, the pain in my arm did not go away. It still went numb on a daily basis and caused me to lose sleep. I started going to an arm specialist, but he did not find any problems. I finally decided to go to a pain specialist, who sent me for another MRI of my neck. The results were a pinched nerve and a bulging disc in my lower neck. The doctor did not think I needed surgery; instead, I received three steroid injections in my neck—during a six-week period—to coat the pinched nerve.

To prepare me for the shots the doctor put me under anesthesia and used an x-ray machine to see exactly where to insert the needle. The first series of shots worked, and the pain went away. For the first time in about a year after my motorcycle accident, I felt good and had no pain in my neck or arm.

However, I had to repeat the process about two years later.

I have been riding motorcycles for over twenty-five years and enjoy many different styles of riding. One of my friends started teaching students how to ride motorcycles. Every time we would get together, she would tell me about the class and students. I thought this was something I would like to do. I began doing research. I needed to find a place that would train me to be a motorcycle instructor. A year went by, and I found a school that accepted me into the program. I had to pay for my books and training material—a small investment.

The training was intense, consisting of four, three-day weekends in a row. The temperatures were in the high 80s and 90s, even reaching over one hundred on one day. Standing in the middle of a parking lot in long sleeves and long pants, I was very hot. Initially, ten students signed up for the program. By the end of the first weekend, two had dropped out. Over the next three weekends, we would lose eight students in all, leaving only two of us for graduation.

The motorcycle I rode was a cruiser-style motorcycle, and it is very comfortable. Riders sit upright, but the downside is that they give up some handling and speed. A few of my friends rode sport motorcycles. That style of bike handled completely different from mine. They were fun to ride but got uncomfortable after about an hour. I remember watching a MotoGP race one Sunday afternoon and thought that would be fun to do. I bought an old sport bike that needed work.

After fixing it and making it road ready, I did some research and found out about a track day. This is where amateurs get to ride their motorcycles on the track, which is a safe and controlled way of riding. Why ride on the track? No speed limit and fewer things to run into. I signed up to do a track day and spent the next few weeks getting my bike ready for the track.

The morning arrived; I woke up at 5 a.m. and drove to the track with my bike in tow. It was a beautiful summer day. As I went through the morning pre-track activities of getting the bike ready, I was getting more and more nervous. I would be in the third round of riders going out. I watched the first group go out to the track, and I was thinking, what am I doing? I got my gear on and got on the bike. As

I drove up to the starting point, I was literally shaking I was so nervous.

The first lap around was very slow, which was good. It allowed me to calm down, and I thought this was not that bad. Then the pace picked up, and bikes were passing me like I was standing still. I just went at my slow pace until the session ended. I got off the bike, and my hands were still shaking from the ride, but I was hooked; this was the best thing I had done in years. The adrenaline was unbelievable. The more I rode on the track the more I loved it. I would go to the track about a dozen times over the next year.

I made the correct choice teaching beginner motorcycle riders. This has been a great source of pride and joy in my life. The Motorcycle Safety Foundation (MSF) program is great. It's always a challenge and surprise on the first day of a new class and then rewarding to see students progress over the next few days. Unlike teaching at college, teaching motorcycles provides instant feedback. Students know immediately if they passed or failed. I see the look on the face of the student that struggles and then figures out how to ride, which is a great feeling.

In the meantime, my father was not feeling well; he was aging and having general health issues. One day my parents told me my father was going to have kidney failure, and that he was going to go on dialysis. He has diabetes, which was the cause of most of the ailments he was dealing with. As time went on my parents were not thrilled with the decision to go on dialysis; he really wanted a transplant. The problem with a transplant is that the patient needs a donor. At age seventy-two, the chance of getting a donor from the list was slim to none. Therefore, I made the decision to give him one of my kidneys; after all, I had two and only needed one. I went to the hospital to get started with the screening process.

I was on vacation with my family when the hospital called me to let me know that I was a match—not perfect but close enough that my kidney would work. I had to meet with several different doctors to make sure I was healthy. I even met with a psychologist to ensure I wanted to do this of my own free will and that no one was forcing me. I assured them that I was doing this to simply help my father, and it was my choice. We did more testing over the next few months and set the date for the end of January.

The day before the transplant a snowstorm arrived, and my parents were not happy, so they decided they would rent a hotel room close to the hospital. I slept at home, woke up early, shoveled out, and then drove to the hospital. There was about three inches of snow, so it took a little longer than normal to get to the hospital. My father and I went into the preparation room. As the nurses were getting us ready, I made sure they knew that I did not want my father's kidneys; he was supposed to get one of mine. They wheeled me into the operating room, and, like all the other operating rooms I have been in, it was cold. Bright lights were on, and music played. The nurses moved me into position, shot in the IV, and I was out.

Lori was there as I woke up in recovery; I felt good. As they wheeled me to my room I was thinking, this is not that bad; there was minimal pain. But that was because the doctors had me on heavy medication, and I did not feel any pain. My father came out of surgery a few hours later. It took longer to put a kidney in than it did to take one out. He recovered well also.

I was able to leave the next day as long as I could walk and use the bathroom, which I was able to do with no problems. Once home, I started to notice that the pain was getting worse. The next few days I was in pain and kept taking pain medication, so it only hurt when I moved. Friday and Saturday were probably the worst days of the pain. I was attending the University of Phoenix for my doctorate at the time. I had actually started a class on the Tuesday before the Wednesday surgery. I was able to attend class and keep on track for my degree, and my papers that week were a little more creative.

One of the medication's side effects was I could not urinate normally. I called the hospital and took other medication but nothing was working. After about two weeks, I went to the doctor to have my bladder looked at. The ultrasound showed I had almost a liter of fluid in me. If I had waited much longer, my bladder could have burst and that would have been very bad. My bladder had expanded to a point where I could not put pressure on it to allow the fluid to come out. He had to catheterize me to drain the fluid out—not fun. The problem was that the painkillers had overridden my sensations of having to go to the bathroom.

That was the easy part. I then had to wear a bag to let all the fluid drain out to allow my bladder to shrink back to normal. It was uncomfortable. After a few days of that, I went back to the doctor to ask if there was anything else I could do. His answer was, "catheterize yourself three times a day." Oh what fun! I did this for about two weeks before my bladder was back to normal. By the end of February, I was feeling like myself again.

Later that year I finished my classes for the doctorate and only had the dissertation to finish, which I began about two years after starting school. The remaining classes were how to write a dissertation and other management classes. I had started collecting data; now the writing was up to me to finish. It was tedious and at times very frustrating. I loved the topic, but it was still dry. I was working on my dissertation over twenty hours per week. Between collecting data, creating questionnaires, and analyzing the data, it was a lot of work.

"A good long ride can clear your mind, restore your faith, and use up a lot of fuel."
Ken Bingenheimer

Then for over a one-week period, I got writer's block. I could not write anything that made sense on my dissertation. In order to keep the time schedule I had set, I needed to continue writing. Therefore, I decided to take a motorcycle trip. I rode to the Blue Ridge Mountains on the Blue Ridge Parkway—for me, the best place to ride and think. It is a 465-mile ride that runs across the spine of the Appalachian Mountains. The trip to get there from New Jersey is about 500 miles. I got on the parkway and started riding. When I came to a spot that overlooked a valley, I stopped, took out my laptop, and wrote until my battery died. I finished more in that three-hour period than I did in the previous month. The next day, I rode again and found another spot to stop and do the same thing. I was now ahead of schedule and headed home. The trip was four days long and extremely needed.

Lesson Learned

My plans changed. I was always working toward being a manager in manufacturing. My focus switched to helping others. While attending many years of college and having some great teachers, I also had some horrible teachers. I thought I could do a better job than those teachers could. At that point, I decided to become a college professor. I became an adjunct and also started teaching motorcycle training.

I helped as a lacrosse coach, not knowing anything about lacrosse; I had to learn the rules of the game. At night between schoolwork, I read lacrosse books to learn about the sport. I would also show up an hour before the kids so the other coaches could teach me.

During that time of my life, I started looking at things that made me happy. The one thing that I enjoyed was helping others to succeed. I had started teaching at a local college and felt like I was making a difference in someone's life. One of my students graduated, and the company I currently worked at—

based on my recommendation—hired him to work in the IT department.

In addition, I was able to put two things together that I really enjoyed, motorcycling and teaching. I went through the training to become a motorcycle coach and am now teaching people how to ride a motorcycle. Helping people achieve their goals or dreams is rewarding.

In order to achieve a goal of teaching full time at the college level, I needed a doctorate degree. The University of Phoenix accepted me into their online program. This was very similar to the format in which I received my master's degree. My goal was to finish in five years.

It was time to buy a house again, as the bankruptcy had cleared. Our goal was to stay local so we did not have to move the kids out of the school system. This meant we would get a smaller house for the money we wanted to spend. After several months of looking, we found the house we wanted. It needed some work, which I was able to do with all that I had learned during years of home ownership.

On my way home from work on a nice day in May, another driver hit me from behind, causing my motorcycle to lurch forward and hit the car in front of me, totaling the bike. This caused ligaments in my shoulder to tear and created a pinched nerve in my neck.

I also gave my father one of my kidneys. We have two kidneys and I knew we only need one. I had some complications with the surgery, but everything worked out fine. My father recovered great and was home within a week and is almost back to his normal activities.

Attitude—I was going through a lot during this time of my life. It would have been easy to get down, and some days I did. However, by this time I knew what it would take to stay positive. Simply believe everything is going to work out and it will. I started looking for the good in everything.

Desire—Up until this point, I was letting life guide me, and I just responded. I wanted to change careers and knew what I needed to do. I knew in my heart and mind that I would achieve my goals. Helping people has become something that I am striving for. The more people I can help the better I feel.

Faith—Going through everything has had its up and downs. There were days I did not know why I was doing what I was doing. I was surviving, but I always felt there was a reason for everything that happened. When my father needed a kidney and I was a match, there was no question that I would give him one of mine. I did not think about complications; I had faith that I was doing the right thing and that everything would work out for the best.

Knowledge—I reached my first goals, but had new plans, so I needed more knowledge. I went back to school to get my masters and doctorate. I had to gain the knowledge to teach lacrosse.

Maslow's Hierarchy—I have stopped switching jobs every few years. We are living in a house and my family is doing well. For the first time in my life, I can look toward the future and not worry about providing for my family. What do I want to do? I want to teach full time and help other people achieve their goals and dreams.

Planning—My planning changed; I had to develop a new plan for a career change. I was no longer pursuing a career in manufacturing; I wanted to help people, become an adjunct teacher, and then become a full-time teacher at a college. I had to get an advanced degree for this to happen.

Reward system – I had small rewards during this time because money was still tight. I would take mini motorcycle trips—that was my reward.

Success through failure—When I first approached Montclair to teach, things sounded possible. However, it took three years of emails and rejections before I was able to teach. Then one year I finally got the answer I was looking for. I became an adjunct teacher at a local college. After two years, I decided to teach motorcycle riding too, and attended a different school.

Time management—I was still working sixty to seventy hours a week. My spare time was at a premium, but I was riding my motorcycle more frequently and taking trips for pleasure. I also started school, so I had to make every second count. Teaching and going to school gave me a place to do research.

Exercises

1. Do something for someone else, give a gift.
2. Help someone do something, pay for a strangers' coffee, pay for a toll for the car behind you. Do something that is unexpected for some else.

Notes

Chapter 8

Rewards

- *Doctorate*
- *Trip*

I went skiing with my daughter to a local ski resort. It was cold and the snow was great. While skiing I caught an edge and fell on my right side. At the time, I did not think much about it and even forgot that I had fallen. A few days went by and my right side hurt. I figured I pulled a muscle or something. However, it was not getting any better, and I was getting worried because it was on the same side as my only kidney. I went to the doctor and told him my right side hurt. He sent me for x-rays and an ultrasound. He could not rule out that it was not my kidney; this did not make me feel any better. After all the testing, he did not know what it was. I went to another doctor, who ran more tests. Nothing there, and again, they could not rule out my kidney. I was getting nervous because at that point, it was a couple of months of being in discomfort. I went to another doctor, who took more x-rays. He found a hairline crack in my rib, and was able to rule out my kidney. I was very relieved, and a few months later, it healed.

While attending the UOP, I had a talented mentor to guide me through the dissertation process. She was extremely meticulous about the wording of my dissertation. At the time, this drove me crazy, making little corrections all the time and sometimes rewriting the same section over and over again.

The collecting and analyzing of the data went quickly. The last two chapters were much better to write, it was all the data and how it affected everything. I only took a few months to write these sections. The next step to completion of my doctorate was the defense of the dissertation. I had prepared a half-hour presentation and practiced for weeks. The total time of the defense was just over an hour, and I thought it went well.

A few days later, I heard back from the committee that it had passed with a few minor changes. I finally submitted the paper to the dean and had six long weeks to wait before hearing if the dean accepted my dissertation. However, in the end this paid off. My dissertation was approved on the second go around, and on May 7, 2011, I received my doctorate. I found out when my mentor called late one Saturday night and asked to speak to Dr. Ferraro. It was such a relief to have finally finished. The journey took five and a half years.

I tried to sign up for graduation in Phoenix, Arizona, but I finished my dissertation too late and missed the cut-off date. That ruined my plans of riding out to Phoenix on my motorcycle. I will have to plan that trip for another time. I was able to be a part of the UOP graduation in New Jersey, as it was only about a half hour away from home. I arrived there and checked in at the registration. Only three people were graduating with a doctorate degree. It was a nice ceremony, and everyone had a good time. For the first time it sunk in, I had finished school and had earned a doctorate.

My two children are a year apart in school, and soon they would both be going away to college. In 2010, my son went off, and my daughter was finishing her senior year in high school—both would be leaving home. I was more excited than sad. The first week was a little hard, but after that initial "getting used to," the house was quiet with them gone. It was nice with just the two of us—no more shuffling the kids around, or interruptions. It was the two of us, just like it was twenty years ago. Christmas came and the kids came home; it was great having them visit. After a few weeks, though, I was looking forward to having them go back to school, so we could have our quiet house back.

This year I had an idea to help some veterans learn to ride motorcycles. I spoke to the owner of the motorcycle school. He thought it was great idea, and he made all the arrangements. We were going to have a free Veterans Day class, where veterans could take the class for free. We had five coaches volunteer to teach the class. We were all very excited.

The day of the motorcycle training class came, and not as many people had signed up as we had hoped for. We were hoping for a full class of twelve, but that did not diminish the coaches' enthusiasm. All of us would have taught the class with only one student because we were committed to helping the veterans. The class went well, and everyone passed.

"You never see a motorcycle parked in front of a psychiatrist's office."
Ken Bingenheimer

Now it is time to start looking for a full-time teaching position at a college. I have started my search. I have been sending out resumes to colleges in the area. I am not sure how long the search will take, and I am not worried how long it will take. I know that over the next few years I will become a full-time professor at a college in the area. It is a matter of time. I will stay at my current job for now until my next new challenge comes along.

One of the reasons why I want to teach full time happened because of the last night of school. It was final's week and I was going to give my final to the class; the campus was completely empty. As I was walking across the campus, a student called my name. He was in one of my classes about two years ago. We started talking. He was on his way to take his very last test before graduating.

He told me that the information from the class he took with me was very instrumental in him getting the job he has lined up. What he learned in class he was able to talk about during the interview process. That excited me, and the next thing he said also made me feel good. He told me that my class was the most fun, and he learned the most in my class. These are the reasons why I want to get into teaching more. I never get this kind of feeling from working as a programmer.

At the end of the ski season last year, I met a friend who is a ski instructor. We spent the day skiing and talking. I had mentioned to her that I was considering becoming a ski instructor, so the conversation turned toward this. I was very interested, but it was the end of the season, and it would have to wait until next year.

Living in northern New Jersey, we have all four seasons: summer, fall, winter, and spring. It is nice to have all the seasons, but as I get older, I do not enjoy the summer much; it is too hot and humid. I love the cold and winter. Therefore, that year, the possibility of becoming a ski instructor could not come fast enough. At the end of October, we had a snowstorm and eighteen inches of snow—it was great. However, it all melted in a matter of days. I thought for sure this meant an earlier winter, but I was wrong. However, I wanted to go skiing over the Thanksgiving holiday, but the nearest snow was about 300 miles away.

October finally came, and I sent my ski-instructor friend an email about becoming a ski instructor myself. She responded they needed more instructors and would email, though it was still too early. In November, she informed me to go online and fill out an application. Then I attended a job fair at the resort and they hired me that day. It was now early December. I convinced my son to do a day trip of skiing, and he agreed. I woke up at 5:00 a.m., but when I went in to wake up my son, he did not want to get up. I asked him what time he had come home, and he said 4:00 a.m. He rolled out of bed and into the car, where he fell asleep before we pulled out of the driveway. About four hours later, we pulled into a Killington ski resort in Vermont. They had over forty trails open. We had a great time skiing together. I was exhausted by 2:30. We left shortly after that for the four-hour ride home. We had a great time, and it was so worth the trip. Over the summer I always think I am a much better skier than I really am, getting out on the slopes always reminds me I am not—a good reality check.

"Skiing is a battle against yourself, always to the frontiers of the impossible. But most of all, it must give you pleasure. It is not an obligation but a joy."
Jean-Claude Killy

Even though there was no snow on the ground, the resort had training for all the instructors because they were implementing a new training method. The method is from Burton Ski Academy, where it was developed and used for the past several years with great success. The method is so simple I do not know why others have not used it before. This little resort in Northern Jersey was going to be the first in the world to try this method on a large scale. We had the training in the lodge; it was quite a site seeing all these people with their ski gear.

The winter was so warm they held the first two training sessions inside the lodge. It was fun and informative. But not having snow was very frustrating. It finally got cold enough for the resort to make snow. We had another training session; I was getting very excited now.

Opening day arrived and I was there to start teaching. I had my first class—seven students of different ages—but they were all beginners. I was set to teach them how to ski. We started out with the basics: this is a ski, and this is what we are going to do. The first twenty minutes went great. Then I took them to the small slope, and it went downhill from there. I had students sliding all over the place. This was going to be harder than I thought. I finally got control of the group, which took about a half hour. An hour into the lesson, two students decided skiing was not for them and left. I had another student that felt like the class was going too slow and left. I had four students remaining. I was able to teach them to ski down the mountain, but it was so much harder than I thought it would be.

I met some great people during that winter at the ski resort. A few things that stood out was the passion of both the guests and the workers. The ski season in New Jersey is very short—only three months, and the resorts in the area need to make a year's worth of money during that time. This season was a very bad winter for ski resorts, having had above normal temperatures and below normal snowfall. Even with the lack of snow, the resort's management did a great job of keeping things positive and keeping us motivated. The enthusiasm of the managers made this a great environment to work in.

    During the season, I trained seventy-five people. Most of them simply learned how to ski and had no real emotion but were happy to do something different in life. However, for a handful of people, it was a life-changing event. You could see it on their faces. In some cases, it was a life-long dream to ski, and now that dream had come true. This was one of the worst seasons for skiing; the temperatures were above freezing, causing rain instead of snow. I think we had less than a foot of snow the entire year. Even with the lack of snow, I was determined to go skiing, so I found snow on the mountains. This snowless year I did the most skiing in one year than any other year.

"Life begins at the end of your comfort zone."
Neale Donald Walsch

I booked a vacation to Whistler Mountain, Vancouver British Columbia for my fiftieth birthday, our twenty-fifth wedding anniversary, and to celebrate the completion of my doctorate degree. Lori and I planned to spend a week there, seeing the sites and skiing. Lori would be going to the spa while I skied. I had booked a day to do heli-skiing on my birthday, hoping for nice weather so the helicopter could take off. I grew up watching Warren Miller ski movies, and this was something I always wanted to try.

Lori and I flew out to Whistler Mountain; the kids were in school and did not come. We arrived on Sunday night, and it rained most of the two-hour trip to the lodge. We checked in and went out to get something to eat. We stayed in the village at the base of the mountain. We ate and went to sleep; the trip was long, and we were exhausted.

We woke up the next morning at 4:00 a.m., as we were still on eastern standard time. The plan for the day was to go on a snowmobile tour. With three feet of snow the night before, it was going to be fun. Lori rode on the back, and we started out slow to get used to riding a snowmobile. Then we turned onto a frozen lake with three feet of fresh snow on it. The guide gave us instructions not to leave a portion of the lake. He had to go back and find two people that were driving slowly.

We were able to ride on fresh snow, in some cases, going airborne. I was an inexperienced driver, and when I went to make a turn, I got the snowmobile stuck in a snowbank. Trying to get the machine out just made it worse, so we had to lift it out of the snow. This was difficult due to the three feet of snow around it and the foot of water under us. My boots were only six inches high, which meant I ended up with a boot full of ice-cold water. We continued on the two-hour trip up to the top of the mountain. I managed to stay on the trails without any other incidents. After a short amount of time at the top of the mountain, we started the descent. We made it back to the starting point with everyone intact. My foot felt like a block of ice, so I warmed up by the fire.

The next day I went skiing by myself at Whistler. My first impression was just how big the place was. They had another six inches of snow the night before, which made for more than two feet of snow over two days. There was powder everywhere and some of the best-groomed trails I had ever been on. I skied the morning and was going to meet Lori for lunch, but she got sick, and we were not able to meet. I skied until the end of the day, trying to make as many runs as possible.

The main reason we came to Whistler arrived: heli-skiing. I arrived at the check-in about fifteen minutes early and then went to the transportation area. I had planned to use my own skis, but once I got there and saw that the other skis were twice the width of mine, I decided to rent a pair. When we drove to the helicopter pad and I saw the red helicopter, my first thought was how small it looked, and I wondered how we were all going to fit in the thing.

We were one of three groups that would share the helicopter for the day, which meant we would be one of the last to get airborne. As I watched the helicopter take off with the others, I was a little nervous knowing that I would be in that thing in a few minutes. Finally, it was our turn, and when the helicopter landed, the windblast was incredible. We loaded the machine, and, in no time, we were over the mountains. The views were magnificent; we could see the entire mountain ranges. As the helicopter set down on the snow, the ten of us unloaded and then waited for the helicopter to leave. Getting our skis on was a lot more difficult than I thought it would be, as we were standing in three feet of snow. Once the skis were on, we started down the mountain.

I have been skiing for over thirty years—almost all of it on the east coast. There is no powder on the east coast, and when there is, it is heavy. This powder was like nothing I had ever experienced. Within the first few turns, my style of skiing was not working, and I fell into the snow. I had to adjust my skiing to handle this new style. It took me the first run to feel somewhat comfortable with powder skiing. We made it to the bottom of the mountain and the lift point of the helicopter to pick up. We loaded into the copter and off we were looking for another place to land.

The second run was a lot steeper than the first run, and the wind had blown the snow, which made the second run very difficult. It was much harder to get into a rhythm and flow down the mountain. There was a two-inch crust on top of the snow. The path we were going down was also much steeper, making for a difficult run. About halfway down the mountain, the crust was no longer there, and it was just soft powder snow. The pitch was still steep, but in the powder, it was a nice run to the bottom. We stopped for lunch at this point. The helicopter landed and brought us a boxed lunched.

After lunch, we were ready for our final run. The helicopter landed just below the well-known "black tusk." This was one of the highest peaks in the area, and we were struggling to get our skis on. As the guide dropped below the hill, I followed, and the steepness surprised me. But the snow was the best yet. This was the best run of the day and most likely of my life; it was just how I pictured it would be–a steep, powder run linking turn after turn.

The last day of our vacation, we were to go dogsledding. We met the dogs and guide, and Lori and I helped the guide hook the dogs to the sled. We were off, and seven dogs pulled us through the woods. About ten minutes into the trip, the guide asked if I wanted to steer. Of course, I could not pass this up. She gave me a brief rundown of what to do, and we were off. The guide gave commands to the dogs and me. I ended up steering about three-quarters of the trip. It was a great experience, and I had a lot of fun. We then made it back to the base station and helped put the dogs away.

Later that night Lori and I went on a horse-drawn carriage ride. It started at the base of the ski mountain and worked its way up to a little shed. Once inside the shed we drank hot chocolate, warmed up, and then went down the mountain. It was a short but very pretty trip; the scenery was great—watching the sunset between the mountains. This ended our trip to Canada, and the next morning we headed back to New Jersey.

Lessons Learned

I completed my schooling and earned my doctorate degree. Even though I am done with school, I will continue to learn new things and continue to study. I want to become a teacher full time at the college level. Currently, we are just getting both of our children through college. I am pursuing other avenues to help people, such as with the fun Veterans Day motorcycle class. I started another adventure of being a ski instructor, which was something I had wanted to do for a long time, but had not had the time to make the commitment. The ski season in New Jersey is very short, only about three months. I am currently working four jobs. However, it is totally different from when I was younger and working three jobs. Those three jobs were simply for money. The four jobs I have today are for enjoyment—the joy of seeing other people succeed. Being a part of someone's struggle and then seeing him or her succeed is a great feeling.

The cracked rib from skiing was not that big of a deal; it healed quickly, and I have not had issues from it. The worry was my not knowing what the pain was and that it was on the side with my only kidney. When the doctor took my kidney, he said I should have no issues unless I punctured it, and that was the first thing that had gone through my mind.

After twenty-five years of attending college, I feel like I am finished; it was a long journey, and I never would have thought it would take that long. I did it one day, one class at a time. It was not that bad; I completed one degree at a time and then worked on the next one. Each time I had set new goals and had different needs. Achieving my doctorate was not a lifelong dream. I was forty years old before I knew that was what I wanted.

We had a big adjustment when the kids went off to college. For the first time in nineteen years, it was just Lori and me at home. At first, it was a little weird with no kids around, but we adjusted quickly. Yes, we missed them, but it was nice with just Lori and me. When the kids came home for winter break, we looked forward to having them go back to school.

Giving back to society is important. The Veterans Day motorcycle was one way. It took the school a lot of work to host this. The turnout was low, but it was worth it. I would do it again and hope to see it become an annual event to help veterans ride.

Being a ski instructor was something I had wanted to do for years, but with my school schedules, I never felt like I had the time to commit to it. This year, with no school, I was finally able to become a ski instructor. It took a lot more time I would have ever believed. In the short ten-week season this year, I worked about eighteen days, which were weekends and holidays. It was so much harder than I thought it would be. Half the class dropped out during the first hour of my first class. But I stayed with it and got much better.

The trip of a lifetime was heli-skiing at Whistler. I grew up watching Warner Miller movies about skiing and always wanted to try it. I thought this would be a great time. It was a reward for graduating with my doctorate, for celebrating my fiftieth birthday, and for our twenty-fifth wedding anniversary. OK, the wedding anniversary, I just threw it in there to get Lori to come. We had a great time. The weather was perfect, averaging 25 degrees, and it was, for the most part, sunny. When the sun was not out, it was snowing—so great weather for a ski trip. There was so much to do at Whistler a week was not long enough, but that is all the time we had. Heli-skiing was the real reason I was there, and it was everything I thought it would be—even more.

Attitude—I have developed a positive attitude toward everything. I am constantly trying to find good in everything and everybody. The attitude will set the tone of how people react to you. Be negative, and people will be negative toward you. Be positive, and people will be happy around you.

Desire—I had desired to complete my degree and I did. Now I am focusing on getting my children through college.

Faith—Faith has gotten me through many tough times over the years, and I know my faith will help me achieve my goals in the next adventures.

Knowledge—I finished schooling, but I have not stopped learning. I am looking at other avenues to help people. I am still reading motivational books.

Maslow's Hierarchy—I think I have reached the top of the pyramid: self-actualization. I have realized what I am good at: helping other people and teaching. My three part time jobs directly relate to this: college professor, motorcycle coach, and ski instructor.

Planning—My planning paid off—I graduated with my doctorate. It was a lot of work, but sticking to a plan enabled me to finish. I did have to make changes to my plan, the length of my plan, and the things I did, but I completed it. I am now looking for other avenues, starting my next adventure, and creating another plan.

Reward system—I am planning my trip to Whistler Mountain to spend a week of skiing. I will be celebrating my fiftieth birthday, earning my doctorate degree, and celebrating my twenty-fifth wedding anniversary.

Success through failure—Not so much a failure, I am now more careful about having only one kidney.

Time management—I am still very busy working four jobs this year: my full-time job, my adjunct teaching, being a motorcycle coach, and being a ski instructor. I still make every minute count and try not to waste any time. The difference between my current jobs and my jobs when I was younger is that now I am helping people and getting personal satisfaction out of them, so they do not feel like jobs.

Exercises

1. Map out how you got to where you are? think about your decisions and why you made them.
2. Have you ever wished you could escape your life for one week? What would you do and where would you go?

Notes

Chapter 9

Wrap up

- *A new beginning*

Why did I write this book? To show that no matter what you encounter in life you can overcome and succeed. I know some people have had it easier than me, and some people have had a more difficult time than I have. That is fine; what is important is that you never give up—you control your destiny. Becoming successful requires work, and it will not come from reading one book; it comes from changing your life and the way you live it. The amount of money you have does not measure your success. Your attitude, and what you deem as success, measures your success. When I was earning my degree, I had so many people tell me that an education is a waste of time and money, and not to bother getting one. But it was important to me.

During my young adult life, I was letting the world control my direction. I had no plan or direction; I did not care, and I only lived for the day. I worked hard but without any direction. I never got anywhere, and many times, I felt I was spinning my wheels. When I got married, I needed to support a family. I could no longer allow the world to dictate my life. I tried to get a better job, but could not because I did not have a college degree. So I got a degree and got a better job. It took fifteen years to get my first degree, but it paid off. Because I did not have a degree, I had to work twice as hard as people who had one did. If you are missing a quality that you believe is holding you back, then you need to know what your strengths are and make them work for you. I worked on making my weaknesses go away, but that took time and effort.

I have used a set of small goals and dreams to reach my bigger goal. When I was younger, my goals were to provide for my family and get a better job. Most of my goals took only three to five years to achieve. Some took longer. But I know that if I had set a goal when I was twenty-five to earn a doctorate, I would never have reached that goal—it was too big for me. I reached that goal by achieving success at different levels of life. Once I reached a small goal, I set a new one. Start with small goals.

Early in my life I did not have any plans, I simply let life push me around, I took what it gave me. I never had a plan for life or was focused. Think of a candle burning, what happens when a breeze blows. The candle will change direction and even blow out. As I got older and learned more, I started creating plans and was more focused on the things I did. I knew what I wanted, how I was going to get it and how long it would take. I was focused like a laser beam. Make your life like a laser beam, be more focused. Do not be a candle blowing in the wind, take control of your life.

I have talked about attitude; it is the most important part of success. Learn to share your positive attitude; find ways to let other people know how you feel. Open a door for someone. The other day, I was in line at a coffee shop, and the person in front of me did not have enough change to pay for the coffee. Instead of being mad, I paid the twenty-five cents. It made the person very happy and it made the server smile. You know the saying that if you pick up a penny (heads up) you will have good luck for the day. What do you do when you pick that penny up and it is tails? Do you leave it there? Turn it over, so the next person can have the luck. Spread your attitude.

You have been given the seed to help you to succeed; it is up to you to put it to work. You cannot rely on anyone but yourself to achieve your goals. Anyone can achieve anything they want; a) know what you want, b) what do you need to achieve it, c) be persistent, d) do not let anyone tell you otherwise, e) every day do something towards your dream.

"A journey of a thousand miles begins with a single step."
Lao-tzu

What activity do you want to do? What are you willing to get up at 4:00 a.m. on the weekend to do?

Besides the core attributes of success here are a few more that you should know about:

Look for the good in people. No matter how a person acts, there is good in everyone. You must find the good, even though many times it will be hard to find. I always assume all people are good until they prove me wrong. I have found most of the time that when I assume they are good, they show their good side first versus showing their bad side first. Take the first step and believe they are good.

Lead by example. You do not have to manage people to lead by example. Do not just ask people to help, show them, and work along side of them. This builds friendship and respect.

Delay gratification. If you put off buying or doing something, you will have a chance to decide if you really want the item. You will also appreciate it more. When you delay the purchase of an item, it will be more special. And you will be able to save money for that item.

Believe in yourself. No matter what anybody says, believe in yourself. Self-confidence is one of the strongest values you can have. When you have a chance, blow your own horn. If you do something great, tell people. However, be careful not to overdo this.

Be persistent. Do not give up; once you set your mind to something see it through. Get in the habit of seeing everything through to completion. If you plan to exercise for twenty minutes, stay and finish.

Have integrity. What are you doing when no one is watching you? No one can take away your integrity; this is something you build and control. To me this is the same as giving your word or handshake. You are the only one that can go back on your integrity. Always do what is best all the time.

Be committed. How committed are you to your goal—like a chicken or a pig? The chicken will lay eggs for your breakfast; the pig will give up his life for your breakfast. Be committed like the pig.

Lesson Learned

During the earlier part of my life, I had no plans, no desire. I only wanted to survive life and provide for my family. As the kids grew up and Lori and I were doing better, I started to understand the power of attitude. For most of my adult life, I read books to help me to succeed. Many of the books I did not understand or simply did not like. But when I started reading them, they planted seeds in my mind. I never had a quick response to anything I read. I never became rich overnight.

I began to understand everything I read, but the most important thing was putting the information to work. I started making a plan, and my time management was getting better. I understood what I was going to do. I did not care what other people thought anymore. I only cared about what I thought.

Attitude—When I was young, I had no idea that my attitude toward life meant anything, and for the most part, I was a typical teenager with an I-am-right-all-the-time attitude. It was not until I was older that I realized the importance of a good attitude. Since that time, I have worked at keeping my attitude as positive as possible.

Desire—What do you want in life? These can be little things, but what you spend your time on is what you are going to desire.

Faith—Have the faith in yourself that you will accomplish your goals. If you do not have faith from within, then you must get it by using a higher power.

Knowledge—As I moved through life, I started to gain knowledge. An important part of knowledge is the ability to know what you do not know. Once you are aware of what knowledge you are missing, you can work on gaining that knowledge.

Maslow's Hierarchy—As I look back at most of my life, I can see where I passed through the different levels of the hierarchy pyramid. At each level, I had different successes and or failures. Once I reached the upper levels, I was able to succeed more often.

Planning—I never thought planning was important. Once I understood that having a plan would help me to complete items, it made a big difference in my life. I learned to organize my life and plan a direction of what I was going to do.

Reward system—Until I was in Amway, I had no idea what a reward system was, I simply bought what I wanted when I wanted it. Having a reward system in place helped me to control my spending and appreciate everything I bought.

Success through failure—I failed many times during my life, but I never let it get me down. After I failed at something in my life, I simply moved on to something else—something that I would succeed at.

Time management—Time management is an essential part of life. Understanding there is only so much time in the day is vital to success. Using that time wisely is also important. How you spend your idle time will determine how successful you become.

Exercises

1. This book planted the seed of success. Now you must provide nourishment for the success to grow. Read more motivational books.
2. Change you attitude, everything can be positive. This comes with reading, thinking and doing positive things to ensure your success grows.
3. Success is a mindset; train your mind to be successful and you will be.

Notes

Recommended books

I believe everyone needs to read as many positive books as possible. If you read only one point of view, it might not click with what you believe. Reading many different types of books will help you to understand how something works.

Building a Positive Attitude, Rich Wilkins
How to be Motivated all the Time, Peter J. Daniels
How to Win Friends & Influence People, Dale Carnegie
Life's Greatest Lessons, Hal Urban
The 7 Habits of Highly Effective People, Stephen R. Covey
The Magic of Thinking Big, David J. Schwartz, PhD
The Way of the Wizard, Deepak Chopra
Think and Grow Rich, Napoleon Hill
Who Moved my Cheese, Spencer Johnson, MD
Why You Do What You Do, Bobb Biehl

Recommended movies

Sometime you need an inspirational movie to get you motivated; here are three of my favorites.

Rudy (1993) Director David Anspaugh
Soul Surfer (2011) Director Sean McNamara
The World's Fastest Indian (2005) Director Roger Donaldson

Quotes in the book

"The difference between a successful person and others is not lack of strength, not lack of knowledge, but rather in a lack of will."
Vince Lombardi

"Victory belongs to the most persevering."
Napoleon Bonaparte

"We learn by doing things rather than talking about them."
St Paul

"Learning is not compulsory...neither is survival."
W. Edwards Deming

"Do what you can, with what you have, with where you are."
Theodore Roosevelt

"Creative minds always have been able to survive any kind of bad training."
St. Bernard

"A man builds a fine house; and now he has a master, and task for life; he is to furnish, watch, show it, and keep it in repair, the rest of his days."
Ralph Waldo Emerson

"A good marriage is one which allows for change and growth in the individuals and in the way they express their love."
Pearl Buck

"A hotel isn't a home, but it's better than being a house guest."
William Feather

"Everyone's a star and deserves the right to twinkle."
Marilyn Monroe

"It is the working man who is the happy man. It is the idle man who is the miserable man."
Benjamin Franklin

"Real integrity is doing the right thing, knowing that nobody's going to know whether you did it or not."
Oprah Winfrey

"If you have knowledge, let others light their candles with it."
Winston Churchill

"A good long ride can clear your mind, restore your faith, and use up a lot of fuel."
Ken Bingenheimer

"You never see a motorcycle parked in front of a psychiatrist's office."
Ken Bingenheimer

"Skiing is a battle against yourself, always to the frontiers of the impossible. But most of all, it must give you pleasure. It is not an obligation but a joy."
Jean-Claude Killy

"Life begins at the end of your comfort zone."
Neale Donald Walsch

"A journey of a thousand miles begins with a single step."
Lao-tzu

ABOUT THE AUTHOR

Salvatore Ferraro, D.M. has realized one of his passions has been to help others achieve their goals. Sal attended college at night for 25 years to earn his Doctorate in Organizational Leadership from the University of Phoenix. He is an adjunct professor at Montclair University.

Sal's enthusiasm for motorcycling and skiing has lead him to teach these two sports and help others achieve their dreams.

If you have any comments or questions please contact me at:
Sal@maneuveringthroughlife.com
www.maneuveringthroughlife.com

Made in the USA
Charleston, SC
29 May 2012